Talk With Me!
**Giving the gift of language
and emotional health
to the hearing-impaired child**

Talk With Me!

Giving the gift of language
and emotional health
to the hearing-impaired child

Ellyn Altman, Ph.D.

Alexander Graham Bell Association for the Deaf, Inc.
3417 Volta Place, N.W.   Washington, D.C. 20007-2778

Library of Congress cataloguing in publication data
Talk With Me:
Giving the gift of language and emotional health to the hearing-impaired child
Ellyn Altman, Ph.D.

Library of Congress catalog card number 87-072929
ISBN 0-88200-163-9
© 1988 by Dr. Ellyn Altman
Published by Alexander Graham Bell
Association for the Deaf
3417 Volta Place, N.W.
Washington, D.C. 20007

Printed in the United States of America

10 9 8 7 6 5 4 3 2 1

Dedication

To Stephanie, a very special person:
For the opportunities she has given me to grow with her.

Contents

Acknowledgments

I thank my family. I thank Stephanie for enabling me to learn how to raise a wonderful daughter who is hearing impaired. I thank Danika for requiring nothing less than the best mothering I could provide. And I thank Alan, my husband, for his support and constant wisdom in the face of the relentless challenges as I tried to give every effort my personal best.

There are several people who gave themselves selflessly to reading and critiquing sections of this book. They generously offered me their expertise and helpful suggestions to make it relevant, meaningful, and readable. I want to recognize them because their spirit, wisdom, friendship, and humanitarianism are present in the ensuing pages. They are Denise Bauer, CSW, mother of a "special" little boy and social worker; Mitch Dicker, systems analyst and personal computer consultant; John K. Duffy, Ph.D., Professor, speech pathologist, audiologist and mentor; Myra Korman, MS, teacher of the hearing impaired; RoseAnn Morris, BA, mother of two hearing-impaired sons and teacher of the hearing impaired; Joseph W. Newirth, Ph.D. clinical psychologist; Patricia Nilson, Ph.D., clinical psychologist; Carol Silverstein, MA, administrator of a school for autistic teen-agers; and Mitzi Weissman, BS, Director of the Great Neck Community School.

I also want to thank my clients who have taught me about mental health--theirs and mine. They include those children and adults I have mentioned collectively and those who have given me permission to describe some of our work together. They have allowed this book to come alive with their real life experiences and to help others learn from their hard won victories. To Lucy Cuzon du Rest, my editor and Director of Publications for the A.G. Bell Association, I give thanks for her vision, creativity, and "labor of love."

Introduction

This is the book I needed twenty years ago when little in the way of hopeful possibilities seemed available to me. I have decided to write it for you from two perspectives: that of a parent, well-seasoned and weathered, and that of a psychologist, well-trained and experienced.

You will read about growing up successfully with your hearing-impaired child through some very hard times. We will explore the events that occur in the life of the hearing-impaired child and all the people involved with the child as they grow together. I know the joy of giving birth to a baby and the anguish of discovering that the baby who appears normal in every way cannot hear. I write this book for my fellow parents because you are the most important people in your child's life. You are not only your child's primary caretaker but also your child's first teachers and most powerful advocates.

I am also a psychologist and my patients trust me to provide meaningful help. So I write also for my colleagues in human service who are also trusted by parents to "care for" and "care about" their hearing-impaired child. Among these professionals are teachers and other educators; mental health personnel such as psychologists, social workers, psychiatrists, and counselors; physicians such as pediatricians and otolaryngologists; and specialists in the areas of hearing and speech such as audiologists and speech therapists.

I also write for family members such as sisters, brothers, grandparents, aunts, uncles, cousins, and friends and neighbors. You will touch the lives of the hearing-impaired child and his parents with a genuine wish to help, confusion about how to do it, and great potential to provide important assistance if informed.

This book is partly a first-hand account -- sometimes a very personal and intimate sharing -- of the challenges facing one family with a severely hearing-impaired child. It is about making decisions and solving problems. It is about emotional pain and dealing with this pain.

However, for the most part this book is about the belief that there is much that a family can do to help a hearing-impaired child achieve a fulfilling, gratifying and productive life. When I first thought of writing this book, I remembered how desperate I had been for help in those early days. Even before the bad news had been confirmed I was dreadfully consumed with fear. I wanted quick, practical, and, if possible, miraculous help. My struggle to help my child is fundamentally what you and I have in common. I learned what **you** will learn as you read my story and we proceed together: from every struggle I experienced you will derive information and strength to tackle the next problem and accomplish the next success.

In the pages that follow you will explore how a baby born with severe hearing impairment can grow steadily into an articulate, intelligent, and emotionally healthy human being. I want to excite you about the prospects for your hearing-impaired child, as I was once excited by one of the first books I read, entled *The Deaf Child* by Dr. Edith Whetnall and Dr. D. B. Fry. They described the "natural" and "normal" development of speech and language achieved by the hearing-impaired children with whom they worked in England. They demonstrated that this development was very much like the development of language in normal hearing children. From this book I developed the belief that if one hearing-impaired child could do it, then **my** hearing-impaired child could too!

There is where I began, and where you can choose to begin also. This will be one of the most important ideas you will read in this book.

Dr. Whetnall and Dr. Fry offered me as a young, inexperienced mother of a very severely hearing-impaired baby a "possibility" that I innocently treated as a "promise"--not a wish or a dream. I had every confidence, that just as they had effectively helped British hearing-impaired children, so too could I help my daughter.

That is exactly what happened. I did help my daughter Stephanie. I helped her achieve the "natural" and "normal" development of speech and language through the use of her residual hearing, her native intelligence, her instinctual desire to speak and communicate, and our shared energy. It was just as Dr. Whetnall had said it would be in a letter she wrote to me shortly before her death. From her invitation to try and my belief in my power to make an impact, I generated an energy from which all Stephanie's growth and progress would follow. This energy grew from a committment to a concept of potential and an invincible optimism. It was based on the determination to fulfill my expectations, my trust in the success of others, and my faith that it would happen, in spite of the odds.

At this time you may be without hope for the future, lacking the faith in yourself and your child that you could overcome this misfortune. I want you to join me and to let me help you learn how to effectively cope with the problems that you face. Come along, you will never be the same. You will discover your power to influence your life and the life of your child.

For ease in reading I have referred to the hearing-impaired child as "he". However, there are as many girls as boys in this group. The following paragraphs will introduce some of the material we will be considering together.

The emotional anguish of determining if your child is hearing-impaired will be our first consideration. We will then consider the subsequent emotional stresses with suggestions to overcome them. We will explore the fundamental concepts that underlie the normal unfolding of language for all people including how you can facilitate this process for your child. This will be followed by a discussion of the hearing aids, including the child and parents' responses to them. We will consider the first steps in fostering your child's development of speech and language with attention to the early "lessons". Then we will focus on the importance of nurturing the development of self-sufficiency by creating enriching experiences. Some specific methods will be introduced to supplement your efforts to help your child learn oral speech and language. In several chapters we will focus on how to foster

xvi   Talk With Me

in your child a mentally healthy sense of self. In these we will consider the impact of the hearing impairment on personality development. We will explore the advantages and disadvantages of being in the mainstream and in special programs. In addition, we will present a detailed analysis of the emotional and social challenges to hearing-impaired children and their families during the developmental periods from birth through adolescence.

My twenty-two year old daughter Stephanie, a graduate student in occupational therapy at Tufts University, will discuss her hearing impairment and her life in the mainstream Her nineteen-year-old-sister Danika and her father Alan will share their thoughts and feelings about growing up with Stephanie. Finally, I will conclude with ideas and recommendations I realized too late to help **my** hearing-impaired child, but I hope early enough for you to help **your** child.

Chapter I

The Wish Not to Know

We are in the bedroom. Our baby is asleep, a musical mobile above her. It is still now. She loves to watch it, as it turns. Does she hear it as well? Perhaps she only sees it move. How foolish the pediatrician is to believe he could convince me that she can hear, when he places the tuning fork at each ear in her full view. Doesn't he know this is more a test of vision than hearing? I am angry that he thinks I am fool enough to accept his ineptitude. I am angrier that he has convinced himself and that he does not have the sense to know better. I am disappointed that he does not have the humility to send me to a specialist.

I argue obsessively with myself. "Did she hear that?" I can't bear to know, but I can't bear not to know.

At eleven months old she looks just fine -- perfect, in fact. Lovely, sweet, friendly, pretty, responsive. It gnaws at me -- this unrelenting suspicion that something is wrong. She screams playfully through the day, but the sounds are piercing. Is this normal? She's my first child. I have no experience. The young mother who lives in the apartment six floors below comments about the shrieks she can hear through the open windows during the summer. Does she know something that I don't? Why does she comment? For an instant I feel she is accusing me of mishandling my child. Why am I feeling guilty?

I remember the "undiagnosed" illness during my third month of pregnancy in the thick of the rubella epidemic. I read everything about the disease. I gave up my teaching job to reduce the risk of catching it from one of the children in my classroom. But I got the "rash" anyway. I saw it. My obstetrician didn't: it was gone by the time I saw him at his office. But no matter, I learned somewhere in all those voluminous reports I insisted on reading that some women have rubella without any diagnosable rash. The damage, if it occurs, is as devastating nevertheless. Reports I read of previous epidemics documented the dreadful effects on unborn babies. I started to worry then.

Here in the bedroom seventeen months later I know I have not yet stopped worrying. Even after I delivered Stephanie and enjoyed a moment's relief to see my baby was not deformed, I did not give up the worrying. I had read the reports, so I knew the verdict was not yet in. I asked the doctor repeatedly about all her functions. He never seemed to understand my torment. He acted as though I wanted something to be wrong, when I just wanted to know. But no reassurance calms me. Now I am in turmoil. Eleven months have passed since I started asking aloud, "Is she all right?" Now I have stopped asking out loud, trying instead to reassure myself.

We visit the opthalmologist. He says her eyes are fine. We visit the orthopedist. She'll wear a wedge on her shoe to correct toeing in. What else could there be? I muster courage to ask about her hearing. I had learned it is among the tragic impairments from rubella. The pediatrician tested what he thought was Stephanie's hearing. But I know he simply tested her vision and perceptiveness. Was I too timid to challenge him, or was I too fearful to go further and really test her hearing?

Then came the breakthrough! A confrontation with firsthand experience. I am in class. Someone asks a fortuitous question about deafness that changes my life. My instructor, a psychologist who had worked in England with hearing-impaired babies, talks about hearing impairment. She is harsh in her indictment of the status of our knowledge. She bemoans how far behind we are in the United States as compared to the British. She describes the work of the British who help the hearing impaired to speak and develop language naturally and normally despite severe and profound impairments.

I wait till class is over. As if I walk a plank, I approach her and tell my story. Calmly but authoritatively she says I must obtain as clear-cut a diagnosis as possible. If there is an impairment, she says, I must know about it immediately and treat it. She stresses how lucky Stephanie is being only eleven months old. If she is hearing impaired and I treat it immediately, she continues to explain confidently, my daughter will be fine. Language will flow naturally. "Otherwise,".... I don't want to think of it. There can be no "otherwise."

I become mobilized, obsessed now with time. The next day Stephanie and I visit the ear, nose, and throat clinic of our neighborhood hospital. The otolaryngologist reports that he can find no physiological abnormality in her ear. He is wise enough to encourage me to explore further and arranges an appointment in the hearing and speech clinic. But we must wait a few days for the audiologist to return from vacation. I can barely wait.

I have been to the library again. I have another book which tells me how to test my baby's hearing. I have been testing all day. It is hard -- almost impossible -- when you do not have a partner or testing team. I can't wait. I gather the materials I will need to make the necessary sounds. Loud sounds like the "boom, boom" of Stephanie's toy drum. Quiet sounds like the crinkle of cellophane and foil. "Tinkling" sounds from the tapping of the spoon against a cup. Musical sounds from Stephanie's merry-go-round and music box. Piercing sounds from the banging of a pot against its cover. Because this is a difficult task and my observations equivocal, I notice I can avoid any conclusions. I cannot be sure I have seen her muscles flinch, or eyes blink, or head turn, or mouth smile, or her body move. I can see testing a baby this way could be very effective because of the familiarity and meaningfulness of the sounds. But working alone is almost as ineffectual as the pediatrician's tuning fork in front of Stephanie's face.

That is why my husband Alan and I are in the bedroom. I brief him on the procedures I have been practicing all day. I tell myself these are the final tests. The most dramatic is the banging pot. Stephanie is taking a nap. I think it is cruel to wrench her out of her sleep with the piercing bang. But I will be so grateful if I can. Alan observes. I can't bear to look. I bang the pot. The sound hurts my ears and the vibrations shock my whole body. Stephanie does not even flinch. She continues to sleep peacefully.

The Turmoil of Suspicion Finally Resolved

Tears fill my eyes and overflow. I realize for the first time, that in eleven months she has never turned when our puppy has barked. She has never heard him. Finally, I know what I could have known all the while, had I been ready. There is something wrong with her hearing.

I know now more clearly -- twenty-three years later -- that I always knew and feared there was something wrong. I have spent hours with friends and patients who have hearing-impaired children and witnessed the same conflict. As a psychologist I know that throughout our lives there are times when it is very hard for us to look because we fear what we will see. But, we must be ready to relinquish our denial so we can proceed with the repair.

It is this conflict about knowing, accompanied by anxiety-ridden, mixed feelings, that is a dreadful impediment to our child's welfare. It intrudes at crucial moments. We must be alert, so it delays us only briefly from responding to the needs at hand.

Parent Advocates: Managers of the Diagnostic Challenges

These are our children. They depend on us as their primary caretakers. One of the binding ties among most of the members of the group I helped organize which came to be known as the New York State Parents of Hearing-Impaired Children was our disappointment and anger with the medical establishment. It was uncanny how one after another of us could tell a heart-rending story of how our child's pediatrician had failed to take the initiative or responsibility for identifying our child's hearing impairment. As a group we informally indicted the medical establishment for inadequacy. In my professional work I still encounter similar themes of medical insufficiency. I continue to resent that pediatricians are still not better trained to take more responsibility for earlier identification of hearing, language, and speech problems for the young children in their charge or even to refer questionable cases for consultation with a specialist.

However, I learned with the New York State Parents group that physicians are simply human beings. Putting physicians into a realistic perspective may have crushed the fantasy of having an all-powerful and all-knowing godlike figure to rescue us in times of trouble. However, this process certainly matured us enough to establish more realistic expectations for doctors. Furthermore, we learned the necessity of assuming a larger share of the responsibility for taking care of our children's medical needs ourselves. Perhaps at the very least we can expect physicians to use their best judgment in applying their training to help solve the problems we bring them and be sufficiently aware of their limitations to send us elsewhere for guidance. And at the very best perhaps we can be grateful if the physician is capable of standing close by to support us through the difficult times as problems are resolved.

In our group we learned the profound lesson Hillel sought to teach in the Roman days almost two thousand years ago that "If we are not for ourselves [and our children], then who will be for us [and them]." The truth is no one can care better for our children than ourselves. We must become our children's best advocates.

I also saw reflected in the stories of my fellow parents that even though frightfully inexperienced, most of us were the ones who identified the problem of hearing impairment for the professional. It is the parent who spends each day with the child and is in the best position to know if there is a condition that should be further investigated. I am not so grandiose a parent to say the parent can make the correct diagnosis. But I am also not so grandiose a professional to ignore a parent's concern, deprive them of taking the lead, or reject them as part of the problem-solving team. Professionals who do not know about teamwork are probably not suited to work with families who have disabled children. In all likelihood, fellow parents, the diagnostic process has begun with us if we have been reasonably attentive to our child. It depends on us to facilitate it with the assistance of competent professionals. Beware, though, that it can be sabotaged by us, our anxiety, and our limited knowledge.

The Formal Diagnostic Process:
What Parents Need to Know

Usually the diagnostic process begins formally when the pediatrician or other physician finally responds to parental anxiety concerning the adequacy of the child's responses to environmental sounds and verbal stimulation. There are probably some very well-informed physicians who monitor their young patient's hearing and language development and bring to parents' attention the need to evaluate their child's hearing, but they seem to be in the minority.

However, it is more common to find that pediatricians make the initial mistake of reassuring parents that their child is just a slow talker. Often they decide unilaterally to wait and see until the average expected age of speech development has passed (between 12 and 18 months) before making a referral for consultation with a specialist. This is a serious mistake, because language development depends upon hearing. Delaying a diagnostic evaluation in order to wait and see if language appears on schedule, is a risk. If your child is deprived of normal hearing, waiting delays the introduction of compensatory auditory stimulation of the remaining hearing and speech and language enrichment. Waiting continues the deprivation.

This disservice results largely because doctors are insufficiently acquainted with the compensatory therapeutic approaches for hearing impairments occurring at birth or during infancy. Parents therefore must recognize, no matter how well intentioned the professional seems to be, that they must act as their child's primary advocate and investigate and question all counsel and recommendations.

Should the parents succeed in obtaining a referral from the pediatrician or another source, they would bring their child to an ear, nose, and throat doctor called an otolaryngologist or an otologist. Some of these specialists have experience with very young babies and children. They have the special skills to evaluate the possibility of impairment. These physicians are interested in identifying any structural abnormalities that can be surgically corrected. They also try to determine if there is a hearing problem due to damage to the inner ear or auditory nerve.

The physician may recommend electronic tests of hearing that have been developed to evaluate impairments in infants and very young children. Immittance audiometry (tympanometry) is one technique that indicates the presence of malfunction of the middle ear.

Information regarding the possibility of a sensorineural hearing loss is also obtained by monitoring the presence of the acoustic reflex. This test is routinely administered in the course of audiometric evaluations to determine if a child has some degree of usable hearing.

Another technique is the Auditory Brainstem Response (ABR) or the Brainstem Evoked Response (BSER). It is similar to the electroencephalogram or brain wave test. Electrodes are pasted to the head and through them electrical activity is recorded and the responses are plotted on a graph. This test is usually administered during the infant's sleep after a meal. At this time the ABR provides only an incomplete picture of hearing, indicating impairments in the 2000 to 4000 Hz range. This procedure requires technical skill to administer which limits its use to hospital centers that own the equipment and employ examiners. Furthermore, it is not administered routinely but usually recommended for infants considered at risk for hearing impairment, including those of low birth weight and with a history of familial hearing loss and prenatal or natal difficulties.

Sometimes physicians or other diagnosticians use less technical tests which employ familiar sounds such as the crinkling of cellophane or the tones of a toy whistle or toy drum. The skill with which these tests are administered and their results interpreted is the crucial element with such testing. Be aware, for example, if the doctor uses a tuning fork, or any of the other techniques mentioned below, that it is a test of hearing and not a test of visual perception that is administered. Furthermore, the child may respond to loud, low frequency sounds, but may not respond to the tinkle of a bell, the crumbling of cellophane, or the familiar tapping of a spoon against a cup. These are techniques used by some practitioners to make preliminary diagnostic judgments about the presence of a hearing impairment. Hopefully, the practitioner who examines your child will have a repertoire of techniques and competent interpretive skills.

If the physician has the slightest suspicion of impairment, your child should be referred to an audiologist who specializes in evaluating young babies and children. This person may also be a speech pathologist as well, and will be able to evaluate the receptive language development, babbling, and other oral behavior which will provide important information regarding the presence of impairment.

Very often the challenge of diagnosing the severity of the impairment prevents innumerable problems. In part, this is because diagnosis is frequently more of an art than a science, even though the audiologist's instruments are highly scientific. Diagnostic accuracy is also a product of experience. The more experience the audiologist has with the particular symptoms, the more likely he is to make an accurate diagnosis. However, a conclusive diagnosis is usually not possible at the first visit.

Often the audiologist performs sound-field audiometric testing during initial evaluations of babies and toddlers. Sounds enter a soundproof room through multiple loudspeakers in which parent, child, and audiometric assistant are seated. The audiologist observes the child's responses to the sounds through a one-way mirror. Subtle cues such as an eye blink or head tilt are sometimes all that are available. Occasionally there may be more dramatic responses such as searching for the source of the sound, a smile or a cry.

A child trained over a period of time in play audiometry, can learn to participate in the testing and provide information about the hearing impairment and the kind of amplification he will need from the hearing aid. The participation in the game usually consists of the child's inserting, dropping, tossing, taking, throwing, or in some way indicating with objects like a ball, blocks, or rings that he has heard a sound made by the audiologist.[1] For example, every time the child hears a sound, he may drop a colorful block into a pail, stack one block at a time to make a tower, or insert one peg at a time into a pegboard. Other forms of evaluation have been developed that use conditioning procedures with novel materials to maintain the child's interest. In response to a sound a child might press the nose of a clown and be rewarded with a token or some form of food. Some testing provides the reward of a lighted picture or a series of puppets that pop up. These have been designed to engage the child's attention through the complex diagnostic procedures. Through these procedures the audiologist systematically tests the child's hearing for the various frequencies or pure tones at cycles per second (cps) involved in speech at varying degrees of loudness or decibel levels. He is able to determine just what sounds are within the range of your child's residual or remaining hearing. He will also be able to test when your child is wearing his hearing aids. In this manner more accurate hearing aid prescriptions can be made.

The diagnostic evaluation helps parents to know something about their child's ability to hear speech. It indicates the presence of

[1] /For your ease in reading, we use pronouns "he" and "his" and refer to the child as "he." Obviously girls and boys are equally indicated in all references.

hearing within the low, middle and high frequencies. For example, some low frequency sounds consist of vowels such as the "a" in father, the "o" in boat, the "a" in saw, and the "u" in blue. These sounds can be heard more easily when there is low frequency residual hearing available to your child. High frequency sounds are characteristic of certain unvoiced consonants such as "s", "f", "p", and "t." These sounds may be difficult to experience for the child with a high-frequency impairment. Since this specific information is not usually available initially from a very young child, hearing aids are usually prescribed by an experienced audiologist based on the child's behavioral responses to the sounds from the preliminary sound-field testing. Therefore the audiologist is more likely to state that there is an impairment, but he may not be willing to indicate the degree of the impairment (e.g., moderate, severe, or profound) until your child can participate in a complete audiometric evaluation. However, the identification of an impairment provides sufficient information to move full steam ahead to provide language and speech training.

Although the initial diagnosis is made and recommendations are discussed with parents, the diagnostic process should not be viewed as completed. Corroboration is important which may involve another audiological evaluation or at least another consultation with an audiologist. Parents are consumers. It is unwise to "buy" the first opinion because you like it or are exhausted from the whole process. I do not say this just to increase your level of stress, but because I want to clarify and emphasize the issues and the challenges. As parents you are also engaged in an educative process. In order to deal with the disability you have to possess as accurate a picture of the problem as possible.

The professional whose evaluation you will adopt is very likely the one who will be guiding you from there on in many ways. This person may be involved with an agency that provides direct treatment such as the auditory training, speech and language enrichment and therapy. The audiologist may make a referral to a therapist and hearing aid dealer. The audiologist may coordinate the efforts of several professionals including the speech and language therapist and the hearing aid supplier. The professional you chose to coordinate the therapeutic services should be your guide until you are sufficiently educated to take greater responsibility.

Choose a person you respect and trust. This person and his or her associates are your mentors and are crucial to your successful and meaningful "growing up with your child." In a sense this person provides the philosophy or orientation to the treatment of the problem in all its aspects from the hearing aid selection to the most suitable therapeutic approach.

These diagnostic procedures and subsequent choices represent the pivotal point for the future. Once the wish "not to know" is confronted and the experience of "knowing" is found to be "not so terrifying," your energy can be freed to start helping your child.

Chapter II

The Initial Trauma

When I was a young graduate student and an even younger mother, I was interviewed for an internship. The interviewer told me that he could see no pain in my life and concluded therefore that I was not prepared for the internship in question. I was hurt, disappointed, and unable to deal with his accusation. Fortunately I obtained a different internship, though it was much less attractive to me. I often wondered why I was unable to confront the interviewer and reveal the experience I was earning in the arena of life's turmoil.

During this time I was investigating my life with my therapist. She tried to help me understand the great difficulty I was experiencing trying to conceive my second child after a relatively easy time conceiving my first. She said the difficulty was related to the trauma of being the mother of a profoundly hearing-impaired child and my fear of having another impaired child. With difficulty I considered her idea, wondering if it could free me from the disappointment from my "infertility."

Those months of infertility were the most painful ones of my life, I thought. This seems absurd now when I compare it to the depth of trauma during those gloomy days of trying to determine if Stephanie was hearing impaired. However, I had always viewed Stephanie's impairment as her trauma, not mine. I only suffered from the guilt of giving her rubella which caused her grave problems. I allowed **myself** none of the compassion I feel toward **other** parents who suffer with their child over any misfortune.

I did not recognize the traumatic effect of Stephanie's impairment on my life. Had I been able to help that interviewer understand how much grief I had experienced, I might have earned the internship. However, this lost opportunity was only a minor consequence of my refusing to face the obvious.

When I refused to recognize that **all** of us -- Stephanie, my husband, and I -- were victims of the rubella virus, I failed to acknowledge a common fact, that in these cases the first ones in need of emotional "first aid" are the parents and other members of the family. They must be treated first, because the baby is dependent on them for care. If I had acknowledged my initial anxiety as part of my trauma, I probably would have forced the medical people around me to pay more attention to my questions. Instead I reproached myself for being an unnecessarily nervous mother. If I had used my anxiety, we might have had an earlier start, which is one of the most crucial factors in helping the hearing-impaired baby.

Respecting Your Feelings and Learning from Them

In my work as a psychologist I try to help people understand how they feel and what they think, so they may solve their problems. Most of these people know much more than they realize. But their knowledge is often not easily available to them. So we dig and search to discover what they know in order to help them.

It is likely you have been more knowledgeable than you have recognized about important conditions affecting your child. You may have had a suspicion that there was something wrong with your child.

Perhaps you have known other children whose early development progressed differently. Or, you may have been aware of a history of disability in your family. Or, perhaps your pregnancy or delivery was complicated. Or, perhaps your baby was ill with a disease that could result in an impairment. Or, perhaps you had no suspicion at all except for the typical parental anxieties about having a "normal" child. Then upon seeing your baby just after birth with no apparent abnormality, your anxieties were temporarily dispelled. Hearing-impairments are usually "invisible" at birth.

Here is the lesson to be learned: do not treat yourself carelessly! If you ever again have a suspicion or a question, investigate it. The only loss may be a waste of time which ends happily in allaying your anxieties. In all likelihood you will most certainly gain information that could be useful.

At best it is many months, but often it takes a year or more after birth, to identify the baby's hearing impairment. Our worst fears, harbored too long, are confirmed. It is important to grieve for the lost hearing and the lost time. Your feelings should not be ignored.

No doubt when you received the diagnosis, the information was crushing. If you had anticipatory anxiety or well-established suspicions, you have probably not collapsed emotionally as you might have if you were totally unprepared for bad news. But, all of us parents suffer deeply in some manner, irrespective of what we anticipate.

Why do we experience emotional pain? Sometimes the disability serves as a personal indictment. Many of us go through life feeling insufficient, inadequate, impaired, imperfect, etc. As a result we may conclude we just passed our limitations on to our impaired baby. Others of us often feel guilty for having done something wrong, real or imagined. We view our baby's impairment as our punishment, and feel that our baby is the innocent victim. Some of us may believe we have directly hurt our child by some specific behavior, like not staying in an antiseptic environment throughout the pregnancy. We might conclude that this has caused the impairment. For some of us it does not matter whether we have done something actually or not to contribute to our child's and our own misfortune. In our conscious or unconscious fantasies we determine we are bad, and as a result our innocent child is abnormal.

Parental distress hurts the parents and deprives their needy child. Therefore, it is necessary to confront the hurt, anger, sadness, and guilt. If we do not deal with these feelings, they can seriously interfere and impede the process of helping our child overcome the handicapping problems of hearing impairment. The problem of dealing directly with these important emotions takes time. For many of us, it requires professional help.

We are probably never going to eliminate our unhappiness about our child's hearing impairment. In time we will adjust and feel less pain. This is largely because the impact of the hearing impairment is probably equivalent to an internal earthquake. The impairment leaves an indelible scar on us, a kind of symbolic equivalent of our baby's disability.

However, there is a very large difference between parent and child. If we are not also hearing impaired, we are not actually suffering from the potentially disabling or handicapping condition. This means that **we** have only to deal with our emotional trauma. All our other resources can be mobilized to help our baby.

This is the reason for obtaining professional assistance: to deal with our emotions. We need to make every effort to save ourselves from falling into an abyss of despair. Realistic goals that can be achieved include dealing with your feelings, accepting the problem and coping with it, and mobilizing yourself to function.

Essentially we want to be emotionally available and actively present for our child. Then we can help him be **only** disabled by insufficient hearing rather than socially and intellectually handicapped by inadequate speech and language. We owe it to our child to come through this emotional trauma. We owe it to ourselves and the rest of our family, as well.

Some Useful Prescriptions To Help You

We may be inclined to ask the familiar question: "Why me?" Some of us are capable of giving a list of one hundred or more reasons why we were chosen to parent a disabled child. Others of us feel totally innocent and victimized. We all need to ponder this question as best as we can with our spouse, family, friends, counselor, therapist, or clergyman. But when your baby needs you, there is no time for self-pity. You will need to put it aside for another time. There is "play-work" to be done with your child. It amounts to a kind of enriching parenting that is the special experience the parent of a hearing-impaired child comes to know and enjoy. To ready yourself for this will take some preparation, achieved by dosing yourself with the following prescriptions.

Prescription #1: The Talking Cure

You will need to deal with your feelings. You want your feelings to assist you rather than disable you. Find a professional with whom you feel comfortable; whom you respect; who will support you through some extended period of time; and who will encourage you to talk about all your feelings without judgment. This could be a therapist (e.g., psychologist, social worker, psychiatrist), counselor, or clergyman.

I eventually consulted with a therapist who listened to me for two years. Not everyone has two years of "stuff" to talk about. However, I have known some parents who have a lot more than two years of talk in them. Although my therapist and I talked about Stephanie, we spent much more time talking about me and my own feelings of impairment. I learned that how I felt about myself would affect my child. Accepting Stephanie with her problem and loving her in spite of it had to start with my own self-acceptance. As I become a more knowledgeable psychologist and wiser human being, I see how obtaining self-knowledge is a lifetime investment of efforts which has paid some fairly high dividends to me and my family.

Prescription #2: Developing a Supportive Network

You will probably need to talk with your spouse and other family members also. Hopefully they will be available. If you have a friend or friends who can enable you to feel better, speak with them too. What you need is to dispense with as much of your unhappiness as possible, recognizing that otherwise it will accumulate and defeat you. Being defeated is not good for your child, because you need to put your energy to work for him. In time you will know less sadness, because you will begin to see results from your efforts. Then you will become your own source of support and reinforcement and need less from others. You may seriously want to consider joining (or starting) a self-help or rap group of other parents of hearing-impaired children who have organized themselves to share information, feelings, thoughts, needs, etc. Remember, two or more people make a group. I helped start a group. It provided me with a multitude of benefits. One benefit was my taking on an organizing role. The opportunity to be effective and helpful made me feel better about myself and reinforced my efforts with Stephanie. It was a general purpose group of mothers and fathers. The education I desperately needed and obtained from the group was another benefit. We heard from educators, researchers, mental health workers, hearing aid dealers, legislators, parents of grown hearing-impaired children, and hearing-impaired adults. Sometimes we had professional speakers who presented differing points of view. Although confusing, they provided the opportunity for choices.

In the beginning my husband and I were confronted with choosing among the oral, manual, or total communication approaches for Stephanie. We learned that the oral approach focused on the development of verbal language and the use of residual hearing and speechreading. The manual approach utilized sign language and finger spelling as the primary means for communicating. The total language approach involved in varying degrees the use of sign language, fingerspelling, verbal language and speech reading for communicating. What we learned from the educators and our fellow parents enabled us to choose what we hoped would be best for Stephanie.

The group experience helped me hear the struggles of the other parents and learn how they coped with their problems and decisions. The group provided me with an opportunity to share myself and my experiences. In this setting I was helped to crystallize my ideas about my "philosophy" of education and prospects for my child. Occasionally, I listened with envy, as I learned of a child's progress which Stephanie had not yet achieved. I found myself challenged by the parent's report to try to help Stephanie accomplish the other child's "success." My optimism was reinforced when hearing of the accomplishments of an older child, because I looked forward to these accomplishments for Stephanie. I held on to the belief that if one hearing-impaired child could do it, then Stephanie could do it too.

I was grateful to these parents for showing me how to help Stephanie even more. In this group of people sharing similar problems there was a camaraderie through which we worked to help ourselves, our children, and each other. Some of these parents have become dear friends. I derive much pleasure as I have followed their children from childhood through adolescence and now into adulthood.

Activity Versus Passivity: Problem-Solving Versus Despair

Prescriptions 1 and 2 focus on efforts to manage the initial period of adjusting to your child's hearing impairment. These recommendations are based on the idea that it is not possible for two opposite behaviors and their accompanying feelings to co-exist. It is just too hard for a person to engage in constructive activity and simultaneously engage in despairing passivity.

Depression frequently results from the experience of loss. Hearing-impairment results from a loss of normal hearing. Whether in parent or child, depression is a reaction to loss. It should be considered a fairly "normal" reaction. However, it should also be treated as an ailment.

One of the best things about reactive depression is that it does not last forever as a debilitating condition. It responds to reparative efforts. All of us will be able to cope with depression, if we can compensate for the loss. Unfortunately, neither the actual hearing impairment nor the subjective feeling of loss will disappear in the successful coping process. However, its control over our lives will lift with every compensatory effort we make. So fill the prescriptions and take your medicine. Start talking! Construct a supportive network! And let's get on with the problem-solving!

Chapter III

Your Child Wants to Speak: You Can Free This Potential Through the Gift of Words

Stereotypes About Deafness: Some Personal Memories

I lived in Brooklyn, New York until I was eleven. Across the street lived a family of two deaf parents and their two normal hearing boys. I did not know the parents. They kept to themselves. I did not know

the boys who were older. They would not bother with "babies" or "girls."
So I watched them from a distance through the years.

I have a vivid memory of the mother running after her sons, calling them to come home. Her voice seemed alien to me because her
sounds did not resemble words. It is more than thirty years later, but
I can still hear her voice -- strained and hollow. Her boys often seemed
to be running away from her, which puzzled me. I felt sad for her. If
she caught them, she would move her hands and arms "wildly" which,
intrigued, but also frightened me. Occasionally the strange sounds
would burst out from her mouth in a jarring accompaniment to the
wildly gesticulating movement of her hands.

My world expanded from the cloistered Brooklyn neighborhood
to the hustle and noise of the subway train. These travels extended my
childhood acquaintance with deaf people. Every now and then a "beg-
gar" would walk through the subway cars and hand my mother a card.
The card said that this person was deaf, unable to speak, and in need
of money. One time I saw a woman do this. I felt more distress than I
did for the men. Occasionally the person peddled pencils, so that there
was an exchange of money for wares. Sometimes two people would
board the train looking much like everyone else. Then suddenly they
would begin to move their hands excitedly, and I would know they were
like the deaf mother of the boys on my block. They were talking to
each other, but I could not understand.

All these people were strange to me. I was without understanding. I had only one stereotype for people who were
hearing-impaired -- the bigotry nurtured in my childhood by my ignorance and fear. I had constructed a stereotype out of my ignorance.
I thought all people with impaired hearing were "deaf and dumb;"
handicapped and unable to communicate normally; with strange-
sounding voices and frightening hand gesticulations; doomed to beg
for charity or work for meager incomes; and likely to have children
who would be ashamed of them. My childhood memories were the
only preparation I had for dealing with my anxiety that my baby might
be "deaf" like those people.

Having a "deaf" child meant I could have a handicapped child.
This was very painful to me. However, I was to have a stroke of good
fortune, because the people I encountered as I began to confront the
possibility of Stephanie's hearing impairment presented another point

of view about hearing impairment. They told me that some hearing-impaired people were able to speak and use language like hearing people, worked at jobs they enjoyed, were not ostracized by the hearing world, had children who did not run away from them, and did not beg for money. I was like a naive child. I had to learn that a baby born hearing impaired might just have a disability, but it could be handled as a series of difficult but manageable challenges in the path to growing up. I learned that a baby was not automatically doomed to be handicapped in speech and language, in social relationships, or in occupational choices.

I learned to distinguish between "disability" and "handicap." "Disability" represented an unfortunate but **surmountable** problem that presented significant difficulties in life, but difficulties that could be overcome. A "handicap" represented a condition that **limited** opportunities, choices, freedom, competence, and success.

The "self-fulfilling prophecy" is the name of a powerful human process. It consists of making happen what you believe will happen by behaving in ways so things happen as you expect. Because I was engaged in a self-fulfilling prophecy, my child is not handicapped by her hearing impairment. She has learned to speak naturally and normally. Her verbal language skill has filled her life with opportunity and choices.

I can admit now, what I could not have easily admitted twenty years ago, without personal shame and embarrassment: the prospect of having a child who would be handicapped was intolerable. It was terrible that she was hearing impaired. But it was unacceptable to me that she would be a victim of a speech and language handicap as well. It was a critical moment in Stephanie's life when I learned that I had a choice of alternatives. My child could live with a hearing disability which would present very difficult, but surmountable problems. Or, my child could be the victim of a handicap, where her opportunities in life would be significantly limited. Victimization by handicap was totally unacceptable to me. If there was anything humanly possible that could be done to erase a handicap, I chose to do it.

It is time now to tell you how the self-fulfilling prophecy works. It is one of the most powerful of human potentials. Then you can decide if you want to employ it for yourself and your child.

The Self-Fulfilling Prophecy

A psychologist named Dr. Robert Rosenthal and his colleague Dr. Lenore Jacobson believed that there is more to learning and achievement than inherited intelligence. They had the idea that while the quality of educational experience was very important, even this was not enough to account for success. They thought success in learning also had something to do with: (1) the expectancies of the teacher; (2) how those expectancies affected the teacher's behavior; and (3) how the teacher's expectancies and behavior intermingled with the learner's potential and attitudes as well.

They set about to test their ideas in a real-life school setting. Early in the school year all the children in an elementary school were given a non-verbal intelligence test. The teachers were told this was a test to predict "academic 'blooming' or intellectual gain." In each class the teacher was given the names of specific children who were identified as those who would show unusual intellectual gains during the school year.

It is very important to note here that these children became part of the group of academic "bloomers" only by chance. All the children who were tested were assigned numbers. However, membership in the group of "bloomers" in each class came from being assigned one of the numbers that appeared in a table of random numbers. Only 20 percent of the children in each class were identified as "bloomers." Therefore, it was simply a matter of "luck" if a child had the right number and **not** a matter of intelligence! However, the teachers believed these researchers. They did not know that the information was not based on test results.

What happened was amazing! Eight months after these children were identified to the teachers, all the children in the school were re-tested. The researchers discovered that the "bloomers" achieved significantly greater gain in their IQ scores than all the other children who were not in the "lucky" group: that is, in the lucky group of random numbers! Furthermore, they discovered that the greatest gains were made by the "bloomers" in the lowest grades or among the youngest children. Their average gain was 24.8 IQ points!

Now this was an experiment to test the researchers' hunch. **They actually demonstrated that attitudes and expectancies have a powerful effect on the performance of teachers and students.** I suspect that because these teachers believed the researchers, they be-

haved in ways consistent with the belief that **these students** had potential. I believe that as a result, these teachers **expected** higher levels of
performance from these children. This was probably expressed in their
interpersonal relationships with the children and the teaching experiences they provided. What the teachers thought would happen did
happen: these students made the gains they were expected to make.
If you would like to read more about this research and the "self- fulfilling prophecy," you can find it under the title, *Pygmalion in the
Classroom* by Robert Rosenthal and Lenore Jacobson published in
1968 by Holt, Rinehart and Winston, Inc. of New York.

It is understandable that this process should be called the "self-
fulfilling prophesy." In a recent meeting of a group of teenage girls
with whom I work, we got to talking about ideas that resembled the
"self-fulfilling prophecy." It got rather heated as they debated the issue
of setting goals and achieving them. They thoroughly enjoyed dis-
agreeing with me and with this idea.

One member vehemently protested that wishing just does not
make an event happen, as she reflected on her frustration at Friday
night parties, where she was feeling rather socially isolated. Then one
of her groupmates wondered if her frustration was related to her hopeless attitude, which was fairly obvious. Before long the girls had
formulated their own variation of the self-fulfilling prophecy. They
concluded that having wishes or dreams was a way of giving direction
to their behavior, which could affect what they might achieve.

Neither I nor these adolescent girls believe in magic. However,
I think we believe in the power of the self-fulfilling prophecy. It can
be explained in this manner. What a person strongly believes can be
so powerful that it gives direction to his behavior. If the person has the
knowledge to reach his goal or fulfill his expectations, the belief and
conviction seems to give that extra **charge** to his behavior to accomplish what he wishes. The equation is:

self-fulfilling prophecy = wish or goal + energy +
application of knowledge and skills = desirable end

My "growing up" with Stephanie and some of my work with other
hearing-impaired people has shown me how this notion of the "self-
fulfilling prophecy" can also have a very powerful influence on the
acquisition of speech, language, social, and intellectual skills by hearing-impaired children. First, parents need to **believe** that their
hearing-impaired child has the **capacity** to develop effective speech
and language skills. There is a very strong likelihood that their child

will be able to fulfill this belief, if the parents **behave** in ways consistent with their **expectations**.

This means that we parents need to cultivate in ourselves the belief that our children can become effective language users. Then we need to educate ourselves with the knowledge and skills to make this happen. Wishing does not make it happen. But wishing it combined with well-channeled energy and skills **does make it happen**. The joy from the small initial successes is so contagious between parent and child that it perpetuates the process. The process is reinforced and thereby guarantees the fulfillment of the prophesy that our children will communicate effectively through speech and language.

What seems to me the most significant impediment to success is the presence of doubt. The teachers believed what they were told about the "bloomers." It is equally important that we parents of hearing-impaired children genuinely believe that speech and language development is the inevitable outcome of certain enlightened procedures. Any doubt will seriously interfere with fulfilling the expectations.

You may question: "What about the children who cannot learn the oral way?" This approach is not necessarily the appropriate choice for all hearing-impaired children and their families. Not only must parent objectives, motivations, and resources be considered, but also the hearing impaired child's temperament and resources. We will discuss this further later in the chapter and in Chapter VII.

Learning to Believe Without Doubt

In my work as a psychotherapist I have no magic. The psychotherapeutic work is long and hard, as anyone who has experienced psychotherapy can confirm. Occasionally there is power in giving good counsel. As a result anxiety and symptoms may be alleviated or beliefs may be altered somewhat. However, good counsel is usually not sufficiently powerful, when a person is in inner conflict about adopting a new point of view or giving up old beliefs.

I had no problem wanting to give up my childhood beliefs about the "deaf," because they were distressing to me. I also had two other powerful experiences that helped to dispel any doubt. At a hearing and speech clinic I met a twenty-four-year-old woman who told me she had a severe hearing impairment. She spoke to me as if she were a normal hearing person. I vigorously interrogated her to discover the secret of her articulate speech and her successful use of language. She told me simply that she thought that her mother's working with her from a very tender age was the reason for her success.

Some months later I met the severely hearing-impaired husband of Stephanie's first infant auditory training teacher. He was as articulate as the young woman and preparing to go to medical school. His opinion about the formula that worked for him was that his parents worked with him on his speech, language, and education every day as he was growing up.

I did not know what all the "work" was about yet. But I had finally seen these living examples of what had only been told to me in the abstract up to that time: that people with severe hearing impairments can have fine speech and language and subsequent opportunities in life. If they could do it, I believed Stephanie and I could do it too!

I do not know what prejudices you bring to your reading. My prejudices might have handicapped me, if I not had the experiences I have shared with you. It may be that you too have had some discouraging acquaintance with deafness. My assurance that language and speech can develop naturally and normally if you learn how to facilitate it may not be so powerful, if you have known a deaf person who is greatly handicapped in his development of speech and language. Despite your wishes to the contrary, it may be that you harbor the anxiety your child will be handicapped as well.

I am strongly committed to the powerful force of the self-fulfilling prophecy. It unlocks energies in us and directs these energies toward our goals. It represents a very purposeful use of human power. However, it could be a valuable but untapped natural resource, like an identified pool of underground oil yet to be drilled. If it goes unused in us, there is a strong chance it will go unused in our children. Getting to use it, however, is not the only way we can help our children. They have other reserves and innate capacities that can help us help them.

The Acquisition of Language: An Innate Capacity

Everyone, including the hearing-impaired child, is born with the capacity for speech and language. This capacity is part of our genetic inheritence which results from the long process of human evolution like other capacities such as seeing, hearing, thinking, and standing upright. Fortunately, the principles of language are part of our innate equipment contained in us like a computer program. This program accounts for each stage of language development.

Speech production involves the speech apparatus which is lodged in our oral musculature. Language acquisition and expression involves the parts of the brain responsible for thinking and hearing. The ability to learn verbal communication is an inborn process that unfolds as a child matures. Most of the accomplishment occurs between birth and six years of age. All of us bring inborn knowledge, language-processing routines, preferences, and assumptions quite naturally to our acquisition of language.

In addition to our inborn capacity to communicate, we have another special capacity involving a need to be effective and competent in our mastery of ordinary skills required for every day life. If you have ever watched a baby, toddler, child or even yourself continuously practice a new skill, you have witnessed first hand the expression of this need for mastery and control of the environment. These skills eventually become automatic functions like walking, eating, writing, throwing a ball, etc. However, we do not start out with a finished product. We begin our lives with preliminary potentials that we practice and combine into complex skillful behaviors.

These two human capacities, to develop language and to cultivate a personal sense of mastery, complemented my hope for Stephanie's future. I became convinced that, however severe her impairment, she was born to acquire language and to master it in order to manage life in her environment.

However, I was not so naive to believe that language simply unfolds magically for the hearing-impaired child. Caretakers must actively guide this unfolding process and set the language and speech mechanism into action. This activity is also necessary for normal hearing and hearing-impaired babies. The activity consists of providing experiences which nurture the inborn language mechanism. For the normal hearing child the nurturing occurs casually in the process of speaking to the baby who hears easily and imitates the sounds, words, and language structures. The nurturing for the hearing-impaired child involves the following three basic "do's" which will be discussed at length in the chapters to follow:

1. Provide adequate amplification in the form of hearing aids.

2. Face your child whenever you speak to be certain your face is in full view.
3. Talk generously about **everything occurring**, focusing in the beginning on observable objects and events.

The Parental Choice: To Fulfill or Not to Fulfill the Prophecy

Once we understand that **we** can foster the fulfillment of the innate potential for language development, we simply have to decide if we are the type of person with the interest and inclination to put the language-acquisition device in gear. This is the business of the remainder of this book. However, before we proceed, we might do well to consider the results, if we do not take a direct and active role in helping. This will permit an enlighted choice.

More than language acquisition will be affected, if we do not choose to enter this nurturing process actively. It is mind boggling to consider how much language is inextricably intertwined with intellectual and social development. Without the use of residual hearing and a useful verbal language system the child is apt to be more than hearing disadvantaged.

Language enables a child to think about what can and cannot be seen. Language allows the child to move beyond concrete experiences that are occurring in the immediate present. It permits the child to consider experiences that have already happened for which he has memories. For example, language enables a child to consider and talk about the trip to the zoo or the visit to grandma's house, what he saw, and how it is related to what he thinks is happening in the present. It gives him and you a chance to share, build on experiences, expand and enrich them, and give further meaning to your lives.

Language allow us to create fantasies or daydreams. It permits the child to move into abstract and creative thought. It encourages planning for the future whether it involves a wish for Christmas, a plan for an invention, or anticipation of an event. Language has the capacity to free intellectual potential in order to manipulate increasingly complicated thoughts. Language is a vehicle to expand oneself.

The social disadvantages growing from language deprivation are equally compelling. It is unfortunate that some severely hearing-impaired people who have not utilized their hearing to learn language are often deprived by others of opportunities in the mainstream, largely because they may seem different or incapable. Some severely hearing-impaired people may even limit their own opportunities by withdrawing from the mainstream, because they lack the language skills, a personal sense of speech and language competence, or sufficient self-confidence. Real or perceived language limitations can result in discrimination and segregation and interfere with fulfillment of innate potential.

Oral language is not necessarily the most appropriate form of communication for all hearing-impaired children. There are other communication systems that provide many of the advantages we have considered above, as well as other benefits. It is important to weigh the alternatives before deciding which system is best suited to your child.

Alternative Communication Systems to Oral Speech and Verbal Language

Every hearing-impaired child should have the opportunity to acquire the verbal language of his culture. However, if verbal language development is too difficult to achieve, it is necessary to make certain the child is not deprived of an opportunity to acquire a communication system that works well for him. I have seen painful frustration, enduring unhappiness, and recalcitrant behavioral problems in language-disabled children caused by hearing-impairment or learning disabilities. These problems occur largely because these children were unable to express what was on their minds. Even when they have matured, the result of early language deficiency is oftentimes lasting inhibition and frustration, insecurity and withdrawal, or explosiveness and destructivenss.

For some children verbal language acquisition may be too difficult. These include children who have not been provided hearing aids until they are well past their third, fourth, or fifth birthdays. Such delay, though much less common nowadays, occurs because their hearing problem was not identified early enough. They have passed the early critical stages when sounds and language develop meaning. For these children using their speech apparatus and residual hearing may be very frustrating and unrewarding.

There are other children whose hearing impairment was identified, but whose treatment was unwisely delayed or very limited until well past their third birthdays. The capacity of these children to use their residual hearing should be carefully evaluated. It may be that they have derived minimal if any benefits from sounds they had heard on which to build useful verbal language from their early experiences.

There are also children whose audiograms suggest they have so little residual hearing that even with hearing aids they would have had great difficulty making sense of sounds. Concluding that a child has insufficient residual hearing for oral language acquisition is a monumental decision, because reliable and valid audiometric testing with a very young child is difficult to obtain.

For the children having great difficulty learning verbal language, total communication may be the most useful means for communication. The total communication system consists of signed English which is a variation of American Sign Language, finger spelling, speechreading (lipreading), reading, writing, and spoken words. The children in total communication programs are encouraged to speak while they sign and finger spell.

Drawbacks to Total Communication

Total communication has gained in popularity because it provides the manual, visual, and auditory means for the hearing-impaired child to communicate. It allows the hearing-impaired child to compensate for his hearing deficiency. It also permits the child to choose the modality and stimuli that work best for him. However, in practice, it usually results in the total communicator's focusing on the manual part of the system.

As a result, total communicators are inclined to become predominantly manual communicators. Verbal language and speech are not usually cultivated and therefore do not become useful skills. This is a very unfortunate consequence for those children who could have developed facility with oral speech and verbal language if they had been given the opportunity to become oral at the start with sign language introduced after verbal skills were well established.

When I speak of "natural" and "normal" language development, I refer to the acquisition of verbal English. Because of the social and intellectual advantages to the hearing-impaired person, I am a proponent of verbal language acquisition whenever possible. I have studied sign language myself and observed the ease with which normal hearing and oral hearing-impaired people can learn it later on. I believe it is desirable for the oral hearing-impaired person to develop manual communications skills after facility with oral language is well established. In this way he can move easily between the "world" of the normal hearing and the "world" of the hearing impaired as well as the manual and/or total communicators.

The Importance of <u>Early</u> "Oral" Education

The process of learning verbal language becomes tedious, mechanical, and difficult when it is introduced to the older child who has not had the opportunity for the natural unfolding of language. Memorizing the meaning and lip movements of every word, learning the mechanics of articulation to produce sounds that are hard to discriminate, understanding words that represent ideas that cannot be seen, and then learning the grammatical and syntactical structure of language are very difficult tasks for the older child. This is the case even if he is intellectually superior with usable residual hearing. Consequently, attempting to teach verbal language, after manual language has been learned as the first language, is an extremely difficult task. It is difficult for young hearing-impaired children to accept this challenge, if they are predominantly manual communicators.

In Chapters IV, V, and VI we will focus on oral training beginning as early as possible in the life of the hearing impaired child. For the moment, however, we are considering the child who has not had the advantage of an early start. It is difficult to decide which approach to pursue when a child is over three-and-a-half to four years old and has not had much opportunity to learn the meaning of sounds and language. I believe such a child should be given the opportunity to become oral, if he has highly motivated parents to help him, professionals that want to assist him and his family, a good supply of residual hearing that is made useful by wearing hearing aids, intellectual awareness, and a useful receptive vocabulary that he "hears" and speechreads. These advantages can compensate for a late start.

If an oral approach is employed with such a child, progress should be closely monitored. Small successes are important and should be carefully noted. Initially this would include the expansion of the child's receptive vocabulary. His receptive vocabulary consists of his ability to understand what is said. This should be accompanied within a period of time by his efforts to imitate the speech he hears and followed by his development of expressive vocabulary. His expressive vocabulary will consist of combinations of sounds expressed consistently. These combinations are words.

These words may not be articulated very clearly, so they may not seem familiar to a normal hearing person. For example, if "o-ee" is used consistently to represent cookie or "ba-e" is used to represent "blanket," the child has words. These gains indicate that important progress is being made, and these efforts should continue.

However, if there is very limited progress in speech and language acquisition after providing stimulation and enrichment, total communication should be employed. It is more important to have a means of expression than to struggle with oral language without success. We want to encourage not discourage communication. We can only urge that each child has a fair opportunity to acquire verbal skill. This can be the door to the world and its wider opportunities.

Another alternative for the child who will not be oral is Cued Speech. This is a system of manual cues which accompany speech in order to remove the ambiguities of lip reading. This procedure will be discussed in Chapter 6.

Concluding Remarks

It is probably clear by now that our beliefs and our values play a significant role in the choices we make and how we behave. If you value opportunity, freedom to choose, and fulfillment of potential, then you will want to provide these for your hearing-impaired child. Limitations in the ability to communicate will restrict opportunities and self-fulfillment. Consequently, it is likely that enabling your child to learn to effectively communicate **orally** will expand his or her life's options.

Acquiring and mastering language and speech skills are your child's birthright, despite the hearing deficiency. A parent with the interest and energy simply needs to learn how to get that language mechanism going. It is a gratifying occupation with abundant and immediate benefits to everyone involved. Once undertaken it tends to benefit all other aspects of life! As you will see shortly, getting it going is good parenting plus a whole lot more -- good parenting -- and the willingness to fully commit and extend yourself!

Chapter IV

The Hearing Aid

The tall man brought us to his tiny office. It was a hot September day. The oppressive summer heat was relentless. The air was still and dense. The three of us amid tall stacks of reports and papers crowded tensely in his cubicle. High above on the wall was a rotating fan, making a gallant effort to rescue us as we gasped for air from the suffocating heat and the compelling anxiety.

She sat tall in my arms, not quite eye-to-eye with this giant of a man. She knew she was the object of his attention. I touched her arm to reassure her, but it was myself I was really trying to calm. She watched the tall man open a box, small like a jewel box. There was a metal object inside, like a jewel. He snapped two receivers into the two earmolds he had made not long before, inserted the prongs of the ends of the wires into the receivers, and attached the end of the Y-shaped wire to the metal box which was the amplifier.

She watched. Curious. She knew this gentle man already. He had dabbled intimately with her ears, making impressions with pink wax ... impressions that would hold in place the receiver of sounds he promised she would hear. He explained that the sound would be amplified in the box, travel upward through the forked wire in order to bring the amplified sound into each receiver that sat in the mold in her outer ears. The amplified sound would travel into her ears, stimulate the nerve cells in her inner ear that remained functional, and travel to her brain through the auditory nerve. Her brain would receive the sounds which she would hear.

With confidence, he explained that if she were hearing impaired, she would permit the receivers to remain on her ears. If she were not, she would pull them off. She cooperated. She could not have known what would follow. But she trusted him. She allowed him to touch her.

With the experience of years sculpted into his face and his self-assured movements, he lubricated the molds and gently twisted them into place. He was calm, and this left me reassured. With deliberation he began to turn the volume control on the box...slowly. We were silent. Only the fan rotated back and forth, groaning as its aged motor tried to stir the stagnant air.

In rhythm with the slow turn of the volume control, she turned her head as if awakening. Searching from right to left and then upwards towards the ceiling looking for something -- for something new -- her eyes sought the sound. She found the creaking fan way above her head and connected this familiar object to the sounds she finally heard. A broad grin broke across her face as she pointed upward with her finger.

I cried with joy, though the moment was bittersweet. I can remember little except my excitement. The tall man affirmed she would pull the receivers from her ears if she could hear without them. His was the final test. The question of impairment was finally settled. Stephanie had accepted the hearing aid.

The Hearing Aid Makes "Visible" the "Invisible" Disability

I had not considered how I would feel about the hearing aid prior to the day we received it and for some time afterward. In large part, this was because our audiologist, Dr. Duffy, had a rather matter-of-fact attitude. There were no choices. Hearing aids were to be worn daily and removed only when Stephanie was sleeping.

Dr. Duffy started Stephanie with only one aid fitted by a Y-shaped wire plugged into two receivers worn on her body in a harness over her clothing. The aid was very conspicuous. We were blessed with the ease with which Stephanie accepted her first aid and eventually the second. With a less severe loss, Stephanie might not have been so accepting of the hearing aids, because her unaided residual hearing would have been more available. Her severe loss was a mixed blessing! I accepted the aids with a childlike attitude of reverence in their power to help.

At first it seemed a little odd for a baby to wear a device more commonly seen on the elderly. Since there was no choice about Stephanie's wearing them daily, I did not consider how I felt about them for quite a while. I simply noticed I had unpleasant feelings, when people remarked about them.

A young child wearing eyeglasses is not an unusual sight. Visual problems are commonplace in young and old alike. The use of eye glasses is widespread. However, a baby wearing hearing aids is rare. The hearing aids announce to the world there is an impairment, inherited or caused by disease. Furthermore, the use of body aids is usually confirmation that the loss is so severe that behind-the-ear aids are insufficient.

The hearing aids are symbolic of deficiency or loss. If we consider our own lives, we can identify some already experienced painful loss or some anticipated, inevitable loss. It is part of our human condition that we become deeply attached to what we hold dear. Consequently, we suffer when we lose what we cherish. The hearing aid is a powerful reminder of "loss" which invariably touches most people. It is a reminder. Examples of possible losses include the death of a loved one; a misfortune like the loss of a job; a loss of function accompanying the onset of a disease like arthritis; or the maturation of our children into adulthood and the emptying of our treasured nests.

The hearing aids can evoke feelings of loss related to imperfection or inadequacy. Those who feel insufficient intellectually, athletically, or socially can relate to how feelings of impairment or inadequacy have interfered with their sense of self-esteem and well-being. The aids may symbolize how helpless we feel facing events such as illness, misfortune, birth defects, accidents, etc. For each on-looker the aids stimulate some response. Aids on an innocent baby, having suffered a loss so early in life, can evoke strong feelings of sympathy, sadness, and identification in the form of personal fear or vulnerability.

In those first years it was hard to deal with well-meaning comments from others about Stephanie's misfortune. The hearing aids seemed to stimulate people to express their own feelings of vulnerability and fear. I believe I also had these feelings. I did not dare experience them consciously for fear I might get detoured from my determination to overcome our difficulties.

However well I insulated myself, I was exposed to a wide variety of human responses to which I had very poor reactions. For example, some "human" comments felt like pity to me: "Poor baby." I learned that this was pity for all of us who are unfortunate victims of circumstances and our own human impotence. But if I had taken time to succumb to self-pity, I suspect I would have experienced an even greater loss -- the loss of valuable time and vital energy.

At other times the "human" comments assaulted me in what seemed inane attempts at humor like, "What kind of radio is your baby wearing?" These were probably expressions of confusion at seeing this electrical device on a baby. Sometimes the comments resounded like an accusation, "Is it really necessary to put a radio on your kid?" I believe this contained suppressed anger at how we can all become victims. In their anger I re-experienced my own anger with the rubella and my own guilt for causing my child this problem.

I received many compassionate comments. These seemed like patronizing attempts at masking the relief that the misfortune had not afflicted them or their loved ones. Undoubtedly I was envious of their good fortune. But I believe I was even more envious of those parents in the New York State group whose babies had more residual hearing than Stephanie. They were lucky enough to wear behind-the-ear aids which could be hidden under their hair.

Having feelings of envy and jealousy were very disconcerting to me in those days. I was taught throughout my childhood that these are not "nice" feelings, and I must purge them from my heart and mind. Re-experiencing these feelings around Stephanie's problem just made me feel even worse about myself. But I could not exorcise them, because I was ashamed to admit I experienced them. I found relief from their nagging intrusion, only when I began to accept that these feelings are part of everyone's emotional repertoire. Hide them as much as we try, we have to reckon with them, if we are to be honest with ourselves and free ourselves from their negative power.

Perhaps you have heard it said, "If lemons are what you've got, then make lemonade!" I believe that is how I resolved my dilemma about the hearing aids and my emotional anguish. I considered that this painful exposure to my own and other people's feelings was a necessary confrontation with normal human reactions. Also, it seemed a necessary indoctrination to how people would approach Stephanie throughout her life until their anxieties, curiosities, and apprehensions were allayed. It seemed to be an important lesson that I should learn to cope with the inquiries and comments which would confront me repeatedly throughout my life with Stephanie. Simultaneously, this process would offer an example to Stephanie who would eventually have to manage the comments on her own. If she were sensitive to being looked at, she too would have to overcome it. She will bear this out in her discussion in Chapter X.

It was a humbling moment when I recognized that Stephanie and I needed to help these people, instead of being irritated, and we too needed to be reassured that this problem was not overwhelming. We both needed our anxiety allayed and our minds expanded. Then others could also accept what Stephanie and I were trying to accept, her hearing impairment.

I became convinced that I needed to educate the "public" by gently confronting my feelings and theirs with information and exposure. Wishing to hide the hearing impairment from view would not have desensitized any of us to our uneasiness. All of us would just have to get used to Stephanie's hearing impairment. The hearing aids remained the symbol of loss, but also an instrument for sound, and they became the instrument to educate others, as well.

Mobilizing Residual Hearing Through the Hearing Aids: The Audiogram

We know that few children are without any hearing at all. The audiologist is the professional who evaluates your child's hearing and arrives at a diagnosis. He determines the extent of impairment. With this information he concerns himself with management of the treatment process. This includes determining which hearing aids will permit the best use of the residual hearing in the speech and language training he will recommend.

The audiogram is a graph of your child's capacity to hear which the audiologist obtains during soundfield testing that we discussed in Chapter I. The audiologist interprets the recorded information and recommends the type of hearing aid that will be needed for your child to effectively utilize his remaining hearing. When an aid is selected for trial the audiologist will evaluate your child's aided hearing and plot the results on an audiogram to determine how effectively the aids are expanding your child's ability to hear.

The audiogram in Figure 1 describes Stephanie's hearing impairment. It will give you an opportunity to learn how to read and derive information so that you can interpret your child's audiogram. The horizontal line at the top contains the frequencies. The frequencies indicate the sound waves which are vibrations, similar to the vibrations created when you pull a rubber band that is held taut.

You might even compare these sound waves to the vibrations of a piano string. When you strike a note on the piano, it hits its attached respective string which moves in a cycle. It will be pulled downward until it reaches its lowest point and then return to its original position. However, the momentum causes the string to continue past the original position back upward until it reaches its highest peak in the upward direction. Then it springs back to move in the opposite direction again.

The sound waves are measured in the number of cycles made in a second. They are measured in hertz. The more cycles made by the sound waves per per second the higher the frequency. We experience the frequencies as pitch and label the pitch as sounding high or low or any variations in between.

KINGS COUNTY HOSPITAL CENTER
BROOKLYN, N.Y. 11203

HEARING AND SPEECH CLINIC

HEARING EXAMINATION

PHONE _____ PARENT _____

DISP. NO. _____ JOURNAL NO._____

DATE _____ LOCATION _____

DOB _____ SEX _____ M.R. NO. _____

NAME *Stephanie Altman*

REF. _____

EXAM. BY _____ AUD. _____

AIR CONDUCTION   BONE CONDUCTION

FREQ	RIGHT	MASK LEVEL	LEFT	MASK LEVEL	FORE HEAD	RIGHT	MASK LEVEL	LEFT	MASK LEVEL
125	NO RESPONSE		NO RESPONSE						
250	NO RESPONSE		NO RESPONSE			NO RESPONSE		NO RESPONSE	
500	95		105			"		"	
750	105		110			"		"	
1000	105		110			"		"	
1500	110		110			"		"	
2000	NO RESPONSE		110			"		"	
3000	NO RESPONSE		NO RESPONSE			"		"	
4000	NO RESPONSE		NO RESPONSE			"		"	
6000	NO RESPONSE		NO RESPONSE						
8000	NO RESPONSE		NO RESPONSE						

Δ Aided Right Ear   O Unaided Right Ear
□ Aided Left Ear   x Unaided Left Ear

SPEECH AUDIOMETRY

	RIGHT	LEFT
AVERAGE AC		
SRT		
MASK LEVEL		
DISCRIM 1		
MASK LEVEL		
LIST / SL		
DISCRIM 2		
MASK LEVEL		
LIST / SL		

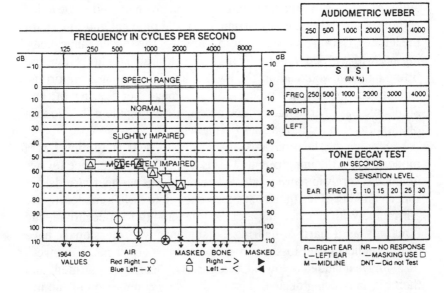

AUDIOMETRIC WEBER

250	500	1000	2000	3000	4000

S I S I
(IN %)

FREQ	250	500	1000	2000	3000	4000
RIGHT						
LEFT						

TONE DECAY TEST
(IN SECONDS)

		SENSATION LEVEL					
EAR	FREQ	5	10	15	20	25	30

R—RIGHT EAR   NR—NO RESPONSE
L—LEFT EAR   *—MASKING USE □
M—MIDLINE   DNT—Did not Test

Figure 1. Stephanie's Audiogram

The loudness of a sound is recorded on the vertical line which represents the decibels. Decibels measure the intensity of sound. Often we experience increased loudness in relation to sounds of higher pitch. The number of decibels required to hear each frequency is recorded on the vertical line. It indicates the amount of amplification Stephanie requires in decibels to hear the pure sounds at each frequency.

You can see that Stephanie's unaided responses (designated by the circle for the right ear an a X for the left ear) extend from 500 hertz through 2000 hertz. This wide response which is within much of the speech range, is largely responsible for the relatively fine quality of her voice. With her right ear she can respond at 500 hertz at 95 decibels; at 750 hertz at 105 decibels; 1000 hertz at 105 decibels; and at 1500 hertz at 110 decibels. Her average loss in her right ear is 103.75 decibels.

With her left ear she can respond at 500 hertz at 105 decibels; at 750 hertz at 110 decibels; and at 2000 hertz at 110 decibels. Her average loss in her left ear is 109 decibels. She is capable of hearing a good amount of spoken language. However, you will notice that her hearing threshold for each frequency level requires high decibel levels of sound.

This requires a very powerful hearing aid. On this same audiogram you can study Stephanie's hearing with her aids. The aided responses are designated by a triangle for the right ear and square for the left ear. Because she heard across much of the speech range, hearing aids with a broad frequency range were desirable for her. However, fitting one that would adjust the level of amplification was important. Too much unnecessary power could damage her fearing further. Stephanie has hearing aids which automatically regulate the amount of amplification for the various frequencies.

Stephanie's hearing aids enable her to hear at the level of a moderate hearing impairment. This is a significant difference for her unaided severely impaired state. When she wears her hearing aids, her speech and her voice quality suggests she might have a moderate impairment. With her hearing aids and her ability to speechread, she functions as a hard-of-hearing person. Many professionals have trouble believing her loss is very severe in view or her performance.

I have included below the categories of hearing impairment and their accompanying decibel "losses." Periodic comparison of the unaided and aided hearing evaluations will indicate the increasing benefits of the hearing evaluations will indicate the increasing benefits of the hearing aids and your child's increasing use of sound. The decibels alone do not tell the whole story. The ability to respond to the various frequencies of sound not only affects voice quality, but the breadth of speech range that can be here. This will help indicate what sounds (high or low frequencies) will need more concentration with visual clues and speech therapy. The hearing categories include:

Normal limits
    10-26 decibels
Mild impairment
    27-40 decibels
Moderate impairment
    41-55 decibels
Moderately severe impairment
    56-70 decibels
Severe impairment
    71-90 decibels
Very severe to profound impairment
    91+ decibels
Stephanie has an average hearing impairment of 106 decibels

The Hearing Aid: How It Helps to Make Sounds Meaningful

The hearing aid is a lifeline which rescues your hearing-impaired child from the isolation of silence and connects him with the world of sound. It brings him into a verbal language community as well as the world of music, noise, and other environmental sounds. The hearing aid is the connector that enhances your child's inter-relationships with his environment and the people in it.

The hearing aid is a vital source of feedback. It feeds back to your child information about his own vocal productions. It enables him to practice what he hears himself produce and to connect these sounds to the physical efforts he has used to produce them. For example, as he engages in vocal play the hearing aids inform him how his mouth, tongue, throat, voice, breath, diaphragm, and lips produce sounds. Depending upon the severity of his hearing impairment, this information might be limited or non-existent without the amplification from the hearing aid.

The hearing aids help him to create a storehouse of auditory and kinesthetic or physiological memories, which he will need when he is ready to speak. These memories are essentially vocal capacities that can be brought forth at will if your child has awareness of them and has had had sufficient practice to reproduce them.

The Baby Learns to Make Sounds: The Beginnings of Speech and Language

All healthy children whether hearing impaired or normal hearing pass through this natural process of learning to make sounds. During the first ten months of their lives at least they engage in increasingly complex verbal activities beginning with gurgling and cooing, babbling and then imitation of the rhythmic patterns and inflections of speech. If the hearing impairment is not identified and hearing aids are not provided, the absence of auditory feedback results in a progressive waning of these critical experiences for listening and speaking.

When Hearing Impairment Interferes with Voice Play

It is here that the hearing-impaired baby becomes more significantly disadvantaged and cut off. The deprivation occurs not only because he lacks the reinforcement or feedback to enjoy the fascination of this vocal play. It is aggravated because he cannot enjoy the reinforcement of his baby-like communications from his caretakers. Hence the hearing-impaired baby tends to withdraw into silence except to communicate his frustration by emotional crying and screaming.

Preventing Impaired Speech and Impaired Listening Skills

According to our knowledge at this time, if this state of deprivation continues past the third or fourth year of life, there is a very strong likelihood the potential to speak and to listen meaningfully will not be realized. The ideal opportunity to cultivate the innate capacity for the natural and normal development of speech and language will have been severely limited and possibly lost. This "loss" is a profoundly handicapping condition. It represents an equal or even greater cost to human development than the examples of losses presented at the beginning of this chapter.

As the normal hearing baby continues this early speech play and babbles in a more complex manner, he begins to reproduce the environmental sounds he hears from the speakers in his environment. At about 10 to 12 months, momentous strides in speech development are observable in the normal hearing baby who has begun to demonstrate the development of his receptive vocabulary. While he may not be able to speak words, he understands them and begins to respond to parental statements, directions, and questions.

Sometime between 12 and 18 months on the average the normal hearing baby speaks his first words. They may not sound exactly like the words used by the people around him, because he is still immature. But the "words" are used consistently, represent some objects (human or otherwise), and resemble familiar words. His articulation may be inexact.

During the second half of the second year the one-word sentences increase to two words and more. The child is practicing the sounds he can make, imitating the sounds he hears, and responding to his family. He experiences personal joy from their excitement, as he begins to "sound" like them and adopt his "mother['s] tongue."

When the hearing aids are used, they permit the hearing-impaired child to resume the process of hearing himself and continuing the natural process of vocal play and imitating others. If too much time does not elapse between birth and the use of hearing aids, the natural and normal development of speech and language will proceed. There might be some delay as the child begins to develop an acquaintance with sound. The process will actually unfold as it does for the normal hearing child. Through his hearing aids the hearing-impaired child hears his own babbling and the sounds around him, imitates what he hears, and practices what he produces.

The Mental Process of Language Development

Simultaneously he engages in the intellectual process of learning language. The initial stage is the development of a receptive vocabulary. The process might be something like this, for example. He may not hear "bottle" the way his normal hearing counterpart does. Instead he may hear "-o--l" or "ba--" or "ba-l." Each time he hears mother's sounds or "label" for the object bottle, he may notice mother brings a bottle. Intellectually he connects the sight of the bottle (object) with the sounds or word he hears (e.g., "ba-l"). Finally he learns that "ba-l" is a sound symbol or word for the object "bottle." This is a conceptual process dependent on his intelligence. The experience including its verbal components is then stored in his memory, as he hears it: e.g. "ba-l."

Before long he may try to reproduce the verbal symbol "bottle" as he hears it "ba-l." His efforts evolve from his previous practice making sounds. He begins to use combination of sounds consistently to call forth or identify this object "bottle." At this point, like his normal hearing counterpart, he too has a word. He may say "ba" or "ba-l." The normal-hearing child may say "badl" which reflects the immaturity of his speech apparatus. The hearing-impaired child may say "ba" or "ba-l" which also reflects his immaturity and his hearing impairment.

The normal hearing child is likely to mature and thereby correctly articulate the "t" sound in "bottle." The hearing-impaired child may eventually need speech therapy to correct or teach the sounds that are missing or distorted. However, this is simply a mechanical process which we will discuss later.

The linguistic groundwork is now established from which speech can be developed and adjusted. **This achievement makes the difference between a hearing-impaired child who will have the ability to use language naturally and the hearing-impaired child for whom verbal language will be a frustration to be abandoned for manual communication whenever possible.**

With Hearing Aids Stephanie Begins the Natural Development of Language

The "scientist" in me kept records of my experiences with Stephanie and the course of her speech development. This was my way of putting myself on a positive reinforcement program so that I could see our progress. Stephanie's first medical evaluation was performed at eleven months by the otolaryngologist in the ear, nose and throat clinic. One week later I met our audiologist Dr. Duffy for consultation during which he evaluated Stephanie and indicated the likelihood of a significant hearing impairment. One week later he took impressions for earmolds.

Finally, during the last week of September on Stephanie's first birthday, she received her most memorable birthday present -- **her first hearing aid**. This gift led to the unfolding of verbal language which was initially fostered by infant auditory training. Stephanie and I participated in the program together guided by an infant specialist and our audiologist. We learned at the hospital and lived what we learned at home.

I made my first entry in my journal approximately six weeks after her first birthday. I wrote that Stephanie was making many babbling sounds which I attempted to spell as follows: "eer," "nema," "la," "ng," "dy," "cch," "gu gu ga," "esh," "th," "nodem." It is notable that several of the sounds are high frequency sounds like "sh," "cch," and "th," which Stephanie may not have even heard. With the hearing aids she could hear sounds with which she played with her voice. I believe her vocal apparatus was being exercised and probably being prepared to produce sounds which were both audible and inaudible to her and necessary for what would become her comprehensible speech.

Eventually she would have to learn to produce these high frequency sounds which were inaudible to her. The capacity to form them kinesthetically had been imprinted during this critical babbling "play time" that skyrocketed in vocal productions once she had received her aids. Furthermore, the piercing screams I had described in Chapter 1 had virtually disappeared. In addition to the "nonsense" words she said, she began to produce two words consistently: "mamma" to designate me and "mow" for her stuffed cat.

From the middle to the end of November, I recorded that her **receptive** vocabulary contained the following words which she repeatedly demonstrated by retrieving the appropriate toys when asked: horse, car, cow, truck, airplane, cat, dog, book, and duck. At fourteen months old, she had increased her expressive vocabulary to include " 'u'" for "up" and " 'am" for "Sam" our dog. By December 4 when asked, she would retrieve the elephant and pig; give a kiss; and point to her eyes, nose, and mouth.

At fifteen months old, she said "bye bye;" "ah ah baby" to put her doll to sleep; "no more;" and "eye," indicating her eye. One month later she had learned that haunting word that eventually torments most parents of two-year-olds, "No!" In February before she was a year and a half, she gave our dog Sam his first command: "Up 'am." Through this month she used "dop" for "stop" and refined Sam's name to "Bam." Just past seventeen months, Stephanie was saying "bod-l a mil'" for "bottle of milk."

At nineteen months, I listed the following in my journal: "Pu' i' ba'" for "Put it back;" "ma bapul" for "my bottle;" "no more;" " 'ome on" for "come on;" " 'ome in" for "come in;" "up" ; "bown" for "down;" " 'roun'" for "around;" " 'i" for "hi;" " 'ot" for "hot;" "daffoo" for "thank you;" "Alan" and "daddy" for her father Alan; and "oof oof" for "dog." It is notable that she was also calling our dog Sam, "Dam." She had moved from" 'am" to "Bam" to "Dam" in her efforts to produce the "s." When she was twenty-one-months-old, Stephanie was speaking in more complex sentences: "Put it back;" "I'll be right back;" and "[Eraser] fell down." At twenty-two months, she added " 'ow pretty" for "How pretty;" "I wa' bo' bown" for "I want to go down;" "Defnie" for "Stephanie;" " 'allo" for "hello;" "updair' " for "upstairs."

Stephanie's vocabulary continued to grow in leaps and bounds. Her hearing aids opened the world of sounds and words to her. Her uncanny ability to speechread, which she taught herself, reinforced her awareness of communication and enhanced her ability to understand. However, it was the human factor that provided the energy and power that led to her success. The capacity of human energy to make a difference will be the focus of our attention from this point forward. We will begin by considering how human energy can be utilized to foster the acceptance of the hearing aids and tackle any problems that may interfere with reasonable goals.

Your Energy Can Overcome the Problems: First, Help Yourself to Accept the Hearing Aids

As you manage the hearing aids it is crucial that you not only appreciate their importance, but also the possibility that you have mixed feelings about them. I have witnessed how unconscious and subtle parental attitudes can interfere with the child's acceptance of the hearing aids and have resulted in delaying their consistent use. Since you have considered the potential interferences of mixed or negative feelings about the hearing aids, it is less likely you will be encumbered by them. It is possible to deal with what you can admit and very difficult to deal with what may be suppressed.

Your Feelings Toward the Hearing Aid and Your Role in Its Acceptance

Problems arise from mixed feeling when we deny them. Under these circumstances we communicate our feelings indirectly and cannot know what our child actually receives. Oftentimes the nonverbal or indirect messages are at odds with our consciously held, verbal messages. It is most desirable that neither we nor others are victimized by our suppressed feelings. We do not want to interfere with the goal of helping our child accept and appreciate his hearing aids.

By the time your child's hearing impairment is diagnosed, you can feel pretty certain that by necessity your child has become an excellent reader of your body language. Body language includes our facial expression which involves our eyes, brows, forehead and mouth. The posture we take with our body and the tension or relaxation of our muscles are also part of our body's language. These are powerful communicators of our feelings, especially when they are strained.

To illustrate, think about the first time you held a baby. Perhaps you noticed some muscular rigidity in your body, a wide-eyed nervous expression, or strain around your month. You may have felt anxious at holding a baby for the first time. After a few moments perhaps you noticed a shift in your muscles. You relaxed. You may have felt better for the baby and yourself as you became more accustomed to the experience.

There may be a close similarity when you approach and handle the hearing aids for the first time. Your body may convey something about your feelings that your words do not. Perhaps when you attempt to insert the earmold into your child's ears, you stiffen and become tight. This is a physical experience that you will communicate to your child. Or, when someone approaches and questions your about the hearing aids as your child watches, you may grimace or frown with apprehension or anger. If you are in touch with yourself and maintain some personal vigilance, you will be aware not only of your feelings, but what your child is experiencing and receiving from you.

If you identify some discomfort about the hearing aids, it will be helpful to consider what possible effect these feelings might produce. On one hand, they nay suggest non-verbally that you find the aids objectionable, disturbing, bad, frightening, etc. Because the hearing aids are of crucial importance in getting the speech and language development process on a normal track, you do not consciously wish for any delay or interference in your child's acceptance of them.

It is important that you remain as aware as possible of your feelings. If you have someone with whom to discuss them, you may be able to resolve these feelings and keep them from interfering with your goals for your child. The process of ventilating your feelings will help immeasurably. Be aware however that you may need more than one opportunity to air your feelings. You may also need some continued assistance at problem solving.

There are specific experiences you can provide for yourself that will go far to ease your own acceptance of the hearing aids. By the time you have reached the stage of readiness for the hearing aids, you have probably met the audiologist more then once. You have become acquainted with his colleagues and program. If you have begun to develop a cordial professional relationship, it is conceivable that the suggestions I will make are possible. If they are not, perhaps some modification may be possible. You want to relieve any of your unnecessary anxiety and facilitate your acceptance of the hearing aids.

Throughout Stephanie's life her audiologist has taken the impressions for the earmolds. This is not always the case. Your audiologist may refer you to a different person for the earmold impressions. Sometimes they are made by the hearing aid dealer or dispenser or his employee or by an earmold production service. The remarks in this section apply to the person involved in making the earmolds whom I will assume for this discussion is your audiologist.

Preparing the impressions that will be made into the permanent earmolds requires that the audiologist handle your child's anxiety more effectively, as well. You can arrange to have a pair of earmolds made for yourself first. You will experience the benign process before your child does, perhaps the best way is to let him watch this. Your behavior will be a powerful message to your child that no words can convey. In addition you will own a pair of molds to help you check that your child's aids are functioning properly. Wearing them will help you experience on some small level what you child is experiencing. Finally your willingness to wear them is an encouraging model for your child, who may be confused about **how important to him these aids are.**

You and you child may also want to observe the process of making earmold impressions on another child who has experienced this procedure. Often children are more reassured by peers than adults. Not only will such observation reassure you child, but probably you as well.

Handling the earmolds initially can be difficult. They are small and unfamiliar. While not delicate, they can be experienced as "fragile." They require some lubrication with any commercially available lotion before inserting. This reduces friction and helps to ease them in the outer ear. Learning the special motion or twist to get a good fit is a skill that may take a little practice.

Eventually, your child will insert them himself. But initially it will be your job. Hopefully the audiologist will demonstrate on your child and teach you this skill. It is beneficial for you to learn to insert the molds on yourself beforehand. Or, perhaps the audiologist can arrange to let an older, experienced child instruct you and let you practice on him. The practice will help develop the skill and go a long way toward allaying your anxiety. In any case, the first time you insert them is likely to be stressful. It is wise to learn how to take deep relaxing breaths so that you can calm yourself when you feel a rush of tension. It is best to do nothing until you can calm yourself.

If you have spent enough time around a speech and hearing center during the diagnostic period, there is a strong chance you have seen little children wearing hearing aids. Absorb the experience and talk to the parents and children. Let you child experience your interest. Talk enthusiastically to your child about the hearing aids he will be getting soon. What your child does not understand from your words will be understood from your body language.

On the day when the hearing aids will be introduced, encourage the audiologist to let you and your child handle the aids. If you have a baby, you may be concerned about the fragility of the aids. **Start teaching the care of the aids from the very beginning.** Use words like "gentle" and "careful" and "easy does it." Let your behavior mirror these words. You will be providing an important language lesson that will build a receptive vocabulary. And do not be concerned that your child does not know these words. He learns them by experiencing you through your behavior and the sounds you make.

Talk To Your Child

At this juncture you may be wondering why I recommend that you talk to your child as if he can understand. The chances are he can understand your body language and maybe even you lip movements. Stephanie never had a speechreading lesson. Even before she received her aids she knew something about communication. This is a skill she cultivated herself. **Do not underestimate your child.**

From the moment you discover there may be a hearing impairment, you should be talking generously to your child. This is the time when your child needs more conversation not less. It is often the time when parents out of grief and naivete simply stop talking to their child. They erroneously believe their child cannot understand. **If you do not speak naturally and normally to your child as you would to any other baby, you will continue his hearing and language deprivation.** Children learn their language because people speak to them. **Children talk to people because people talk to them.**

Once your child has touched his aids and explored them visually, it is time to insert them...gently, calmly. Hopefully you will have had some practice and your child is not entirely a guinea pig.

We do not usually reach our goals without some difficulties. I have attempted to troubleshoot the potential pitfalls that could interfere with your goals for your child. It is now time to focus on you child to determine what problems he might present in the process of making the earmold impressions and wearing the aids.

Problem-Solving: Helping Your Child To Accept His Hearing Aids When He Is Anxious About Them.

By the time the aids are actually introduced you and your child will have hurdled some difficult challenges. These can become limbering exercises for even greater challenges to follow. If each of the steps you have taken went relatively easily, consider yourself very fortunate. However, if your child becomes resistant by the time you arrive at the earmold-hearing aid hurdles, you will need a positive problem-solving attitude to resolve the difficulty.

The Importance Of A Problem-Solving Approach

A problem-solving attitude indicates that you believe you will solve the problem **one way or another sooner or later** with patience, **creativity** and every maneuver you can muster. With any other attitude you are vulnerable to becoming too anxious and losing sight of your goal: to help your child accept his hearing aids.

For example, under stress you might take an authoritarian or dictatorial approach. You might try to force you child to "cooperate" or, you could become so overwhelmed with your resulting helplessness that you would simply extend your child's deprivation by your inactivity. Furthermore, if you are unduly stressed you could find yourself subject to the anxiety of others around you. You might feel reproached by the professionals for not giving them a cooperative patient. You might even become victimized by a well-intentioned relative who suggests some dictatorial maneuver or some permissive advice to leave your child alone. Neither will be good for you or your child in the long run.

Are you wondering what magic could possibly come from this "problem-solving orientation?" I will explain the procedure first. Then I will illustrate with the potential problems parents might encounter. First, you need to define your goal so you will be able to recognize if there are obstacles in its path. If there is some interference then you have a problem. It is helpful to identify the conditions either in your child and/or in the situations that are frustrating your efforts.

Then you will want to generate **as many alternative solutions** for the problem as possible by **brainstorming** yourself or with helpers. At this point you just want as many solution as possible. No evaluation is used **initially, reject no potential solution, no matter how absurd or impossible**.

Once all the alternatives are listed, you want to consider each alternative and the **consequences** of employing each one. This is an evaluation process. From here you will **select a solution** or plan of approach that seems best suited to your needs. Then you will **execute the solution** and take careful **note of what happens**. If you do not reach your goal, them it is back to the drawing board to select another solution from the alternatives, based on whatever new information you may have uncovered. Or, you may need to brainstorm again to come up with a new set of options.

Sooner or later you are going to solve the problem. Later on in this book we will refer to this problem-solving approach as a means of working cooperatively with your child to solve problems. But at this point, without a preliminary foundation, including a problem-solving vocabulary, you cooperators are likely to be relatives, friends and professionals, rather than your child.

How to Proceed

Now we will try to apply this procedure. There are several different scenarios that could frustrate you and your child at the time of taking earmold impressions or introducing the hearing aids. There are problems in need of quick and practical solutions. For example, let us suppose your child refused to lie still for the audiologist to make the earmolds. He cannot wear hearing aids without earmolds. For a body-type aid the hearing aid receiver snaps into the earmold and the earmold fits firmly in the outer ear. For the behind-the-ear-type aid the earmold has a tube which leads to the hearing aid.

Making this impression is a very precise task. If the impression is not an almost perfect fit, there will be feedback of squealing sounds from the aids. We have all heard this from a microphone which is too close to the loudspeaker. If the earmolds are not a good fit your child will not get the full benefit of its amplification, and there will be an unpleasant feedback noise.

If your child is not cooperating, your goal is being frustrated and you have a problem. You may try to analyze the problem by asking: Why isn't my child cooperating, lying still, and allowing this person to make these earmold impression? It is important to recognize that at best you will generate hunches. These are guesses that result in the creative process of generating a solution.

For example, perhaps your baby is frightened by this stranger, because he is at a normal developmental stage of fearfulness of strangers which occurs in the last quarter of his first year. Perhaps you baby is just simply afraid of unfamiliar places and would behave this way no matter with whom he was confronted. Perhaps your baby is active and reacts to any restraint with resistance. Or perhaps your baby is hyperactive and does not have the neurological capacity to lie completely still while awake. Perhaps your baby is teething, or developing a cold, or just having a bad day.

There are probably many other possible hunches. Inherent in these considerations are some possible solutions. You will need to select which of the possible problems might apply to your child in order to know what solutions you want to employ. If your baby is ill, it certainly makes sense to delay the appointment until he recovers. If your otherwise happy baby is teething, you may want to obtain some medicine to numb the pain or delay the appointment. If your child tends to be very active; but can be still for a brief period, perhaps two appointments are indicated. Also the audiologist can have his materials ready so with no delay, an earmold can be made at each appointment.

Are You Parent-Centered or Child-Centered?

What if your baby is afraid? You certainly would not want him to associate his earmolds, ears, hearing, or hearing aids with a traumatic or anxiety-filled experience. Fear is often a component in any resistance. You will need to consider you child, his preference and peculiarities, and dip into your knowledge to create a means to calm and reassure him. This is a completely child-centered task.

A parent-centered task is very different. A parent-centered approach occurs when the parent tells the child how to behave and expects the child to cooperate with the parent's directives. This often results in disappointment for the parent.

Being Child-Centered: The Road to Successful Problem-Solving

When I researched the elements for successful acquisition of speech and language by a group of hearing-impaired children, I guessed that it had something to do with the parenting they received. One of the variables I studied was how their parents were centered in their interactions with their children. I asked: Were they parent-centered or child-centered?

I learned that the mothers of the more competent children were child-centered and paid very close attention to their children's temperament, behavior, and feelings. They used this information to enable their children to cooperate. The mothers of the less competent children were parent-centered and expected their children to do what they--as the authority figure--directed. Their children tended to be resistant or withdrawn and less articulate.

By child-centeredness I am not advocating letting your child do whatever he wishes. This would be akin to spoiling (hurting) your child by not providing appropriate discipline. We will discuss this further in Chapter VIII. I am recommending that your child be viewed as and individual with right to have his feelings seriously considered before anything is requested, expected, or imposed on him.

If you are willing to consider the importance of child-centeredness, then you can proceed to solve the problem of your child's possible fear which maybe interfering with the progress of making the earmolds. No one knows your child better than you. However, you need to be willing to brainstorm, using your awareness to find a solution. For example, increased familiarity with the procedure may foster his cooperation. You may need to take your child to the audiologist's office several times before the earmolds can be made. The audiologist might be willing to spend a few minutes with you and your child just becoming re-acquainted and perhaps give your child a treat when you leave. You could supply the treat which could be a small toy.

During these visits it may be helpful for both of you to see impressions for earmolds being made on another child who is being cooperative. Even if your child did not openly express fear, it probably would be reassuring to witness the earmold making before it actually takes place. You might even have one of your earmolds made during on of these visits, saving the other for your child's earmold appointment.

At home this experience can be played out with a doll, if your child is old enough. This imaginary play process is one you will engage in repeatedly for fun and to expose your child to speech and language. This would be a good use of this kind of play. You can use a doll or two dolls (one for you and one for your child) and play out the experience with clay or play dough the actual color of the waxy substance used by the audiologist. On another day you can play out the experience on each other.

By the time you get to the audiologist for the impressions, you and your child will have vicariously de-fused a potentially threatening experience and will be ready to more actively assist the audiologist. Furthermore, in the play preparation there would be a lot of talk and drama which will focus attention on communication and you will have begun the language-stimulation process.

Perhaps all that may be necessary to allay your child's anxiety is to plan an easy morning before the appointment . Hopefully you will be able to schedule this appointment at your child's best time of day. You may also plan a pleasurable or easy time for yourself in order to keep yourself calm.

When your child is brought into the room, if this is the first visit, you may want to show him around. Hopefully the audiologist might join in and show him some of the tools he uses. In this way the room, the tools, and the audiologist can be associated with good feelings. You might have your earmold made first. Taking turns is a way of modeling or setting an example for your child to follow.

Perhaps giving your child some of the wax to manipulate while wax is placed in his or your ears will help. Manipulating a soft clay-like substance can be soothing. It may help to stroke your child's hair to let him feel your presence.

If you find the audiologist is impatient and/or unwilling to deal with your child's anxiety, you may need to discuss this with him. If he is unwilling to alter his approach to your child, you may consider finding another audiologist. However, if the audiologist is cooperative and your child is still anxiety-ridden, you may need to discuss with your pediatrician the use of a light sedative to calm your child. This is a last choice, because it fails to include your child in the process to work through his fear directly and mature through it. It could leave a residue of fear that will be attached to the hearing aids.

Reasons Children Reject the Hearing Aids and How to Solve the Problems

The principles of familiarizing your child and working toward the reduction of unnecessary fear also apply to the introduction of the hearing aids. If your child accepts them initially, again consider yourself and your child fortunate. If your child refuses or removes the hearing aids, it is important to question how appropriate the aids are to your child's hearing impairment. Could they be too loud? Could they be insufficient and provide no real help? Once this question is considered and settled, you can start inquiring into other reasons for their rejection.

Imagine yourself having to accept a foreign object into your ear, when you were young and had no understanding of the reasons. Your child may need a good deal of input to comprehend the advantages to him of wearing the aids. If your child has a significant loss and discovers a new world of excitement and interests with the aids, he will have no trouble accepting them. I have known children who fought to keep the aids on when parents tried to remove the aids at bedtime. Some children who accept the aids sometimes just need a break from them for brief periods. Their need for time out should provoke no anxiety in you. The break time should be treated with the confidence that your child will put them back on after a little while.

Rejection becomes a problem if your child has a significant impairment and does not appreciate the aids at all. In this case you will want to help your child learn to love sounds and thereby associate the aids with pleasurable auditory experiences. Once again your creativity will be called upon to determine what your child enjoys, so that you can associate wearing the hearing aid experience with other already established or soon to be established good experiences.

For example, if your child likes to visit the zoo or the park, plan a trip with the hearing aids. Little children can understand the idea that the hearing aid would "feel bad" if it is left behind. Do not fret about whether your child will understand this. You will need to become expressive which will enable you to communicate ideas such as these through your body language, "acting out" until your child has the receptive vocabulary to understand.

For some children, the hearing aids become an immediate part of their bodies. For other children, an educative process is needed to enable them to move from seeing the hearing aids as a potentially threatening or annoying object to a good friend.

On the other hand, your child's developmental stage may explain his rejection. Here is an explanation to consider. Some resistance simply occurs with chronological age. Around two years old many children become negative and enter a period called the "terrible two's." Your child's developmental challenges which he will grow through could be responsible for his rejection of the aids rather than genuine unhappiness with the aids. (See page 142 for further discussion.)

You want your child to wear his hearing aids throughout his waking day. However, if there has been a problem with immediate acceptance and you have tried to solve it, your progress can be monitored by noting if the aids are worn one minute longer than the time they were worn before. Wearing them as long as they were worn the time before is holding on to already accomplished growth. If you are having this problem, it is a good idea to actually record the amounts of time involved. This awareness will enable you to keep track of your progress and help you feel encouraged.

Now if everything you try is a failure, you need to play around with outlandish solutions. If you believe that wearing a hearing aid yourself would enable your child to accept the aid, then it is not absurd to try out this solution. No absurd solution should be rejected, if there is a chance it might get you to your goal. The only reservation should occur when a solution. No absurd solution should be rejected, if there is a chance it might get you to your goal. The only reservation should occur when a solution would be unfair to someone.

When I wanted Stephanie to learn the concept "upside-down," I stood on my head. I did whatever she needed me to do to help her understand. I eventually discovered that she was capable of hearing even when I was not directly facing her. That was because she had learned to take any position she needed in order to see and communicate with me. There is something special in a relationship where you and your partner will do whatever is in your power to master a problem. The result is that at twenty-three, few problems seem capable of defeating Stephanie, in spite of the great difficulties she often experiences.

In short, your child's future is in your hands. Be assured he will go the distance his potential will allow, if your are willing to lead him through the first miles of the journey. And the first mile after diagnosis requires acceptance of the hearing aid. You need to get his momentum going. Once your child starts, there is no stopping the process of growth. **Growth is inherent in the nature of emotionally and physically healthy human beings.**

Chapter V

Creative Parenting

For longer than I like to admit I believed that Stephanie's hearing aid compensated for what her ears could not hear. In my fantasy she was able to hear almost normally with the aid. I even told this to curious people, and no one doubted me. During the early days I was very naive about the hearing aid, and also very ignorant about how I could help her hear with it.

At the beginning I was without any assistance. Stephanie and I had been sent home with very powerful medicine in the hearing aid but no directions on how to make use of it. I did know how to put it on her and adjust it, but I had no idea about how to stimulate her language. There was one consolation: I was assured that within a matter of weeks we would be assigned an infant auditory training teacher who would teach us.

However, I was determined not to waste any time. I did not know what to expect of the critical period of language development, but it seemed very serious that not a waking moment be lost. My intensity and motivation were so great that in the eyes of an observer I may have seemed like a borderline fanatic. nevertheless, with a fairly clear head I turned to the only sources of information I had: Dr. Whetnall and Dr. Fry's book *The Deaf Child*[1] and a letter from Dr. Whetnall. Both book and letter contained the same message:

1. Be certain to have your child wear her hearing aids at all times during her waking hours.
2. Be certain to face your child whenever you speak to her.
3. Be certain to talk, talk, talk to your child.

Rules 1 and 2 were explicit. I could follow them because Stephanie accepted her hearing aid, and I was able to face her whenever I spoke. Rule 3 was the big challenge. How does a mother talk to her hearing-impaired baby? What does she talk about?

After talking unself-consciously to Stephanie for her first eleven months, I was suddenly lost. Everything we did had become very serious.

Out of necessity and fairly quickly I discovered that the mother of a hearing-impaired baby talks in the most creative way she can. She wants to stimulate her baby's interest in her, because she is the carrier of speech and language. It is uncomplicated: the mother does everything she can and uses every available resource to attract her baby's attention.

Enrichment and Readiness: "Verbal" Interaction WITH Your Hearing-Impaired Child

When the hearing aids are introduced, your child begins to learn about sounds. During this initial stage, talking with your child is devoted to stimulation and enrichment. You will want to help compensate for missed or insufficiently experienced opportunities by

---

[1]/Whetnall, E. and Fry, D.B. (1964) *The Deaf Child.* London:G.Heinemann.

providing an abundance of new and novel experiences. Therefore you will talk **with** your child whenever possible.

Why is talking so important? Early in your baby's first year he began to play with his body and become acquainted with it. Like normal hearing babies he played with his voice: gurgling, gooing, and babbling. Sometime during the latter part of his first year, when he could not hear his vocal play, he began to vocalize less. In time his vocal play may have all but disappeared except when he was emotionally stressed.

If his development had proceeded normally, you would have imitated his sounds and responded to his newly developing speech as he babbled. His babbling would have sounded increasingly similar to your speech, as if he were echoing the sounds he heard. Most parents play the imitation game with their babies. It provides feedback to the child about his vocal mechanism and what it is capable of producing. It also imprints into his memory bank the fundamental sounds that form words. These would have become the kinesthetic memories your child would eventually retrieve in order to reproduce the words he heard.

Unless he received hearing aids and language stimulation during his first year of life, the natural development of language was probably interrupted for your child. However, once the hearing aids are placed on your baby the natural process should resume. If we can attract his interest and if his residual hearing is being stimulated with the assistance of his hearing aids, babbling and imitation should evolve.

Child-Centered Means Talking WITH, Not AT Your Child

Initially, auditory stimulation is the goal. Be certain to talk as much as possible to your baby. Speak with the intention of interacting **with** your child, rather than talking **at** him. Start speaking in "goos" and babbles of your own that you would have spoken had the early process not been interrupted. You want to help him pick up where he left off. **You want to talk to him to make up for his lost opportunities.**

Speak so that the joint experience of verbal "interaction" is communicated and enjoyed. When he begins to vocalize, repeat his sounds so he can hear them from you too. You will give his sounds validity so that they will be imprinted in his auditory-kinesthetic memory bank for use later when he will construct words.

For example, the baby playing with the gutteral "g" as in "goo goo gaa" is preparing a skill to be retrieved spontaneously or with assistance in speech therapy. From this babbling will come words such as "go" or "good." If you sense he is making an effort to communicate meaningfully, respond to his sounds with words of your own, words that may approximate the nonsense sounds he is producing. Or, respond to his "words" with what you think he might be meaning from the existing circumstances. For example, he may be babbling and playing with his fingers and sucking on them with pleasure. Say to him "Bobby's fingers taste so good, yum, yum." You will give him words that he will return to you someday. Showing joy and pleasure when your child gurgles, goos, and babbles reinforces his interest in language. His pleasing you, pleases him and makes him feel very powerful!

This interaction between you and your child lays the groundwork for speech and language. In my study of hearing-impaired children and their mothers, there was a striking difference between the children very competent in speech and language and those who were less competent. The more competent children interacted with their mothers verbally: they exchanged ideas. The mothers of the less competent children tended to dominate the conversation, speak incessantly without pause, nag, and lecture. By dominating the interactions they gave their children much less opportunity to express themselves and practice their speech and language. As a result, these children were less able to express and explore their ideas and communicate skillfully.

Through this initial period the babbling will begin to change. Eventually, your child will use sounds consistently to refer to an object, a person, or a situation. The sounds may resemble words you have used. In fact the sound combinations that are used consistently are words. Your child will have begun to communicate with shared language. The most important thing to do is encourage it. You may be inclined to correct or try to improve the new words. **Do not!**

However, you can feedback your pronunciation of your child's word -- confirming that it is a shared word and offering your pronunciation as an acknowledgment. For example, it is not uncommon when a baby learns the word "up" for him to say, "U" as he reaches up to you. It is not unusual for a parent to say, "Not "U" say "**up**." However, it is more desirable to say something like, "Tommy wants to go **up.Up** you go!" as you pick him up.

This provides correct pronunciation whether heard through the hearing aids or seen on the lips. It comes without criticism. It is important to remember, your child's articulation may be a reflection of his immaturity, insufficient practice, and/or hearing impairment. It is true you will want to get good speech habits going as soon as possible. **Early criticism, however, will suppress his pleasure in speaking**

Natural Speech Development Depends on Hearing Natural Speech

How we speak often conveys attitudes we have about ourselves and about the person with whom we are speaking. If you believe your child is destined to learn to speak naturally and normally, then you are likely to convey just that by speaking naturally and normally yourself. It is most desirable that your manner of speaking with your child is the same manner you would use with any other child his age who does not have a hearing impairment. However, there are some special considerations.

The Importance of Being Playful!

Since you want your child to be able to see your face, you want to talk without moving too much. However, if you hold yourself as if you were wearing a strait jacket, the chances are you are not going to be much fun to "listen" to. Speaking to a child with a deadpan expression is dull for the child. Any child, but especially your hearing-impaired child, needs to be with a "live wire" that is going to ignite excitement in a world filled with interest.

Watch people who enjoy little children and babies. They are easy to identify. They tend to "forget" themselves and speak with expressions that are full of enthusiasm, warmth, and affection. They seem to be able to make contact with a little child from the little child that resides within themselves. As they play they use nonsense words and concoct endearing terms just for the child.

This freedom to play becomes a very important element in your relationship with your hearing-impaired child. It is not only more fun to be uninhibited as the parent of a hearing-impaired child, but it is more interesting to the child. You definitely want your child to find you and what you have to say interesting because the best learning experiences grow from play and a good time.

It is not necessary to yell or talk very loud because your child has a hearing impairment. The hearing aids are worn to amplify sound, so you can relax your voice. You may find yourself exaggerating your speech and your lip movements to insure your child will get your message. This is undesirable for several reasons. It is offensive, because it suggests you have limited expectations for your child. It does not take too much observation for your child to notice that he is the only one with whom you speak in this way. It will not add to his sense of self-esteem for you to talk as if you do not expect him to hear or understand. In addition, others will observe you and imitate your example. They will talk to your child as if he lacks any hearing and intelligence.

However, it is equally undesirable to speak without voice because you know your child's hearing is limited. This common error deprives the hearing-impaired child of sounds of which he is already deprived. Not only does your child need to hear the specific words you are saying to the best of his ability, but also the rhythm, inflections, and every other subtle nuance that communicates meaning.

It is very helpful to talk with your child at his eye level. Bending down, lifting your child to your eye level, or perching him on a stool or table will put you face-to-face. Attention is more easily obtained and maintained this way.

Early "Lessons" in Speech and Language

By now, you are probably wondering what the parent actually does to help get the language and speech mechanism into operation. All the efforts described above are part of the readiness process. There are specific activities that will be helpful to your child. Before discussing some of them, it is important to summarize some the basic principles which should be part of every experience you provide for your child no matter how old or how sophisticated he is.

1. Try to make your interactions pleasant and playful.
2. Try to give admiration and any other form of positive reinforcement for your child's efforts.

3. Try to orient your time with your child toward some purpose:e.g., spending fun time together, having an adventure together, or sharing more structured experiences such as learning a new concept, word, or sound.

At the beginning you want to provide extensive opportunities for your child to exercise his vocal mechanism. He needs to expand his memory of sounds to produce sounds spontaneously and imitate sounds he hears and sees. These sounds will become the equivalent of funds in a bank account from which your child will be able to withdraw his verbal resources when needed to say words or correct his speech.

It is desirable to foster correct articulation as soon as possible so that bad habits are not practiced. However, you will want to do this in a manner that is constructive and non-critical. You can accomplish this through play by expanding the repertoire of sounds your child can produce.

One method is playing with "animals" and their sounds. Children like animals and relate to them. If you have a pet, you have a head start. A dog or a cat are wonderful assistants. At various times in our home in addition to our dog Sam we had guinea pigs, a rabbit, gerbils, and hamsters. They helped me teach a great deal including speech and language. If I could not get Stephanie to attend to my words directly, I managed to tickle her interest with what I was saying to Sam or what I thought Sam was saying to me.

In addition to having pets you can begin to collect inanimate three dimensional animals of any size. You might also regularly visit the nearest zoo and farm in your area. These on-site experiences and the conversations, pictures, and stories that develop afterwards at home can lead to lots of conversation.

Almost every week until Stephanie began school at three years we made a trip to a zoo in New York City. The trip was never boring, because there was so much to do. In addition to the animals there was time for lunching, snacking, and purchasing a souvenir. Muscles were exercised by climbing on curbs and benches and running in the open spaces. Sometimes new friends were made.

When the animals were the focus of our attention, there was much to talk about. Each one had a name. When they made their sound, we would imitate them. The sounds they made were sometimes more important than their names, because Stephanie could more easily imitate these sounds at first. The animals were fun to watch because they had funny, scary or interesting behavior. Whatever they did, I would talk about it with Stephanie and offer her new words to accompany the action.

If you have a toy model at home for each of the zoo animals, it is possible to play "zoo" just about anytime. It is especially good on days when the weather is inclement, your child is ill, or it is just more convenient to be indoors. You can bring out your ever increasing collection of animals, reconstruct the zoo experience or create some imaginary play, and use their names and their sounds. The lion may arbitrarily roar like "rrrrrrrr," the tiger might arbitrarily growl like "grrrrrrrrrr," and the monkey might "ch ch ch." In the play you will also be practicing articulation. The sounds will be needed eventually for the "r" in "rain", the "g" in "girl," and the "ch" in "church." If the animals do not have a familiar sound, make up a sound. You simply want to encourage your child in the imaginary play to use his voice, the animals' names, and the previous experiences at the zoo that will help you share experiences and language.

Relating Imitation of Movement to Imitation of Sounds

Furthermore, children love to mimic animals. They are eager to somersault like the monkeys, prance around like apes, lumber around swinging their trunks like elephants, squirt water like hippos, fly like birds, balance on one leg like flamingos or slap hands like sea-lions. All this physical activity involves verbal interaction and descriptive words. The play experience provides the opportunity for you and your child to "talk" together while using the three dimensional animals, memories, and motor play to recall the fun.

In support of providing enriching and fun experiences for children, I am reminded of the mother of twins who was complaining of her twins' lack of cooperation, her nagging, and her yelling at them. The father noted that whenever his wife issued a directive that was followed by the promise of some excursion outside their home, the twins immediately cooperated with her requests! Many children do not mind the "tedious" task if there is something special that results as a consequence.

Importance of Self-Sufficiency and How to Nurture It Creatively

After a few months of mothering my hearing-impaired child, I had become immersed in the process of stimulating residual hearing, speech, and language. I had learned a great deal from Stephanie, from her auditory training teacher, from some literature I received from the John Tracy Clinic, and from other parents. I no longer felt naive or ignorant.

When Stephanie was between a year-and-a-half and two-years-old, I had an experience that would affect everything I would do with her afterward. I had agreed to participate in the Rubella Project being conducted by a team at the New York University Medical Center. It was an intensive study that investigated all aspects of development of the victims of the rubella epidemic.

While Stephanie was being observed, I was interviewed by a social worker who asked me many questions about my life with Stephanie. One section of the interview consisted of questions on hygiene. This is what I remember of this part of the interview:

Social Worker(SW): At what time of day do you bathe Stephanie?

EA: In the early evening before dinner.

SW: Tell me about what you do.

EA: She and I have a wash cloth. We share the soap and together we bathe her.

SW: Who fills the tub?

EA: I do.

SW: Who determines the temperature of the water?

EA: I do.

SW: And the depth of the water?

EA: I do.

SW: Now tell me about dressing?

The interview proceeded with other questions of this sort. There were no comments about my answers from the social worker. After the interview I found myself preoccupied by the bathing questions. I wondered about all the times I said, "I do." Was it necessary for me to do all that I did for Stephanie? Was I interfering with the development of her self-sufficiency, self-confidence, and self-esteem by doing what she could probably learn to do for herself with some assistance?

I concluded that it was a good thing for Stephanie to learn to fill her own tub, to learn to judge what temperature she wanted her bath water, and to learn to decide what was a good depth for the water. We could continue sharing the bathing process. However, I could help her learn to prepare the bath and do a thorough job of washing so that eventually I could withdraw to let her bathe herself.

All of this was done through communication. I would talk about and show her as much as possible before she removed her aids. Even though her aids were off while she bathed, she would speechread. I knew she understood because she had heard and seen the words beforehand and she also interacted with me. In addition to learning to care for herself, she was exposed to many new words and concepts.

We could share the cleaning up because bathing had become a partnership. Bathing was no longer just a routine activity. Instead it had become a partnership which fostered cooperation and responsibility. I have never forgotten the effect of the social worker's questions on me. From this experience, my efforts to help her become a successfully self-sufficient person evolved.

Considering Adjustments in Life Style

Dedication to your child's growth during the critical stage of language development is essential. Until your child is three-and- a-half to four-years-old, it is likely his development will be your main or one of your main priorities. By four years of age the fundamental work will probably have been accomplished. Then you will probably delegate increasing responsibilities to professionals such as nursery school teachers. Parents usually relax somewhat from the intensity that was formerly necessary.

What follows in this and the next section may be somewhat disturbing to you. I offer the ideas for your consideration and **not** as prerequisites for success. The efforts you extend in behalf of your child **must** be in harmony with your needs and personality if you and your child are to benefit from them. In order to creatively and successfully "parent", **you must** establish the ground rules by which **you** can live.

Here are some considerations which could make your life a little easier.

During this critical period you might want to imagine that your child and you are involved in an intimate partnership, cooperating in the processes of living, sharing, and helping each other. You may take a child-centered approach when you are together. This means that you will seriously consider your child's maturity level, interests, temperament, and capacities in your daily efforts to enrich his life and facilitate his development of speech and language.

Because you will be extending yourself with great dedication during this period, you could feel stressed by the needs of your child. You might even feel overextended and neglectful of yourself. You must attend to your own mental health to sustain your creative energies. It is necessary therefore to provide some parent-centered attention, as well. You can provide this for yourself by arranging for as much personally meaningful relaxation, pleasure, and rewards as possible.

Consequently, housekeeping may become less of a priority. You may even consider engaging a person to assume primary responsibility for keeping house. If there are other children in the family, you may feel it is helpful to have assistance from extended family members like grandparents, teen-age nieces and nephews, aunts, and uncles. If a relative is not available, perhaps services from a domestic helper, a mother's helper, or an "au pair" might be obtained.

Even the attention formerly invested in your marital relationship might undergo some modifications during this critical period. The amount of time and energy your spouse and you have for each other may be transferred in part to sharing responsibility for your hearing-impaired child and other children. Being sensitive to this adjustment and its consequences is important. While you may have to relinquish quantity, there is no reason to give up the quality of your leisure-time activities together. Your shared devotion to your hearing-impaired child may bring you closer together. However, it might have a negative impact and stress your marital relationship at a time when your emotional support of one another is crucial. In such an event some problem-solving may be needed with the assistance of your professional family counselor.

You may even consider altering your family plans during this period by postponing having another child for a while. It is very important for your hearing-impaired child to have siblings. However, children require lots of attention, and you may not want to deprive any of your children attention during their critical early years.

Your commitment to your hearing-impaired child requires careful planning so that other family members are not neglected. It is possible to attend to everyone's needs including your own, but it will take forethought and planning.

An Example of a Day in the Life of You and Your Toddler

I have created an example of one kind of day you might consider spending with your hearing-impaired child. When two friends and colleagues of mine reviewed this section and offered me their reactions, I thought about eliminating it. One reviewer is a social worker and parent of a "special" child with a significant genetic problem, and the other is a teacher and the parent of two congenitally profoundly hearing-impaired young men.

The first one kidded with me and said playfully though pointedly, "If I didn't know better, I would have been certain you were flying "high" on some kind of drug when you wrote this section. Were you serious!...You don't believe mothers can actually have this kind of day with all the other responsibilities they have?" The second said kindly but advisedly, "Of course, you mean this is an example of just one kind of day. You agree that sometimes you can have a meaningful time just being quiet at home. Right?" Both my friends on their own admission were somewhat overwhelmed, by this imaginary day.

Each of these women have been dear friends for a great many years. But neither they or any other of my friends witnessed my days with Stephanie. These were private affairs. With embarrassment I reluctantly confessed to my "critics" that life with Stephanie was much like this imaginary day--very active, stimulating, demanding, gratifying, and --very, very exhausting. Their responses, however, inform me that what you will read may seem to you unrealistic, unpalatable, and unacceptable and/or curious, stimulating, and interesting.

Often, the extent to which some people will go toward realizing their goals may have a disturbing effect on our sense of adequacy. We might even find ourselves disconcerted and asking why we are not behaving like them. At those times we may feel uncomfortable with the comparisons we make between them and ourselves or the competition we may feel. For women more so than men, competitive feelings often exist in a latent or suppressed state. As little girls we are taught that being competitive is "not nice." If competitive and envious feelings arise in us, they may be very disturbing.

Like all of our other human emotions, they can be very useful. However, we need to acknowledge and deal with them. Freeing these emotions will also free the potentially useful energy that had formerly been used to suppress them. This energy can then be used in behalf of our own goals.

Instead of eliminating this section therefore, I offer this imaginary day as an example of a way to share time meaningfully with your child. Some twenty years after the fact, it still does not seem to me an unreasonable way to spend time with your child, especially if you are committed to the self-fulfilling prophecy of natural and normal speech and language development. I recognize that there are many other meaningful ways to spend time with your hearing-impaired child. This is not offered as a yardstick for comparison but as a possibility for your consideration.

The parent I have described (and was) has no other major daytime responsibilities besides her hearing-impaired child. In this example we join this mother in her stream of consciousness.

It is Tuesday night and your two-year-old is asleep. You have had a very demanding day, are tired, and can barely keep your eyes open. However, you know you will be better off if you think about tomorrow tonight and make some tentative plans. The weather report calls for a mild fall day. It is outdoor weather. You went to the zoo on Monday and to the speech center for language enrichment therapy today. The lesson revolved around vehicles--trucks, cars, fire engines, boats, etc. What do you want to do tomorrow?

You can take it easy and go to the neighborhood playground after lunch and swing your child on the swings, slide on the sliding pond, do the seesaw, and let him play in the sandbox. There will be other children, some parallel play, perhaps some positive interaction, and maybe some surprises. Or, you can take a walk to the neighborhood firehouse, look at the fire engines, and even talk to a firefighter. You could take along the new firetrucks you just bought. Then tomorrow night you can read the story about the firehouse. Or, you can just take a walk in the park, pick clover and count the leaves, and see if any buttercups are in bloom yet. You decide to decide in the morning, now that you have some thoughts that are of interest to you, which will probably interest your child as well.

Wednesday morning your child sleeps late. What will you do with the unexpected time. Linger a bit longer in bed? Join your husband for some breakfast before he leaves for work? He has gotten into the habit of taking his own breakfast and eating alone to give you less to do in the morning when your toddler needs attention. Today you will sit and chat with him while he breakfasts. You are very aware that your time together has been significantly reduced by your child's needs for both of you during this critical period. You notice your husband appreciates your joining him. You will eat with your child, since this has become a routine and an opportunity to share an experience involving lots of talk.

A half hour later your child is awake and you greet him cheerfully. You are very glad he is in a good mood. Sometimes he is cranky in the morning making your life miserable. He is still in diapers, but you have begun to talk to him about using the toilet like mommy and daddy. You know you will be in the talking stage for many more months. He gets you the diaper, and you talk about what you are doing.

You both go into the kitchen to decide on breakfast. You take out a few possibilities and each decide what you want, all the while talking about the decision. Together you prepare, eat, chat, and clean up. At two years your child has a receptive vocabulary and some expressive vocabulary that you can understand. You notice much of the talk is on your part. You monitor yourself so that you do not dominate the "conversation". You listen carefully to his utterances and his body language, giving feedback about what you think he is saying.

He does not protest your feedback, so you are probably translating his words fairly well. Then it is time to dress. This too is a little project, just like breakfast. You tell him about the weather report, check the sunshine with him through the window, and discuss what to wear. You give him two choices. He decides and together you dress him, encouraging him do as much as he can himself.

You do not have a regular housekeeper. Your once-a-month cleaning service is not scheduled till next week. You bought your child a toy vacuum cleaner and encouraged him to get it so you can vacuum the apartment together. You both begin. He gets bored. You are losing interest too, but you are not finished. You decide to try to finish, so you ask him to help you push the big cleaner which interests him for a few minutes more. Off he goes to the toy chest. You finish the rugs and decide that is all the cleaning for now.

You want to review the lesson from the clinic and you notice he is playing at the toy chest. This may be the time to take out the new firetrucks you bought and go through the excitement of opening up a surprise package and adding them to the collection of vehicles. At this point you decide to take the walk to the firehouse.

You tell your child about what you will do in the afternoon. With genuine enthusiasm you talk about the firehouse, the firemen, and the firetrucks. You get the book and show him the pictures. You and your child play with the vehicles. You both build a highway and a garage for them out of blocks. As you clean up with him you ask him for the vehicles by name, giving him a chance to learn and practice what he knows. As a child you did not go to nursery school, but you have a feeling this experience resembles what lies ahead for your child next year. You prepare lunch together, giving your child an opportunity to take some responsibilities. Then you get ready to go out.

You start your walk to the nearby firehouse at one o'clock. You use the stroller so your child can walk and ride. Along the way you talk about the vehicles you see, the colors of the flowers along the way, and anything else that catches your child's or your eye. At the firehouse you talk with the firefighter who boosts your child up to climb on the fire engine. This is the best part of the adventure. Your child really enjoys using his muscles.

At three o'clock when you return home, you notice both you and your child are tired. He goes in for a nap, and you plan your free time. You pick up a book, read for a while, make a phone call to a friend. The rest of the afternoon is spent on bathing, giving the bathroom a quick cleaning while your child is playing with some water toys in the tub, dinner preparations, and giving him dinner.

Daddy arrives home and plays with him for a half hour. It is his day to read the story. You have told him about what you did, and he agrees the story of the firehouse is a good one. Your child is tired and accepts going to sleep even though he would like to play some more with daddy. Finally, you are alone. You and your husband have a late dinner, talk about the day's events, and clean up together. You are as tired tonight as you were the night before. You certainly have full and demanding days and earn a very good night's sleep. As you unwind, you begin to consider some possibilities for tomorrow...

Planning a Special Event for Each Day: Maintaining Your Child's and Your Own Interest

When you arrived at the firehouse yesterday you thought you would see some trucks and some firefighters. Instead after you arrived and did see what you expected, the unexpected happened. An alarm went off and the firefighters had to mobilize, take out the firetrucks, put on their raincoats, sound the alarms for the auxiliary fighters and take off. It was all exciting and unexpected. The sirens were loud. There was an abundance of auditory stimulation. You and your child had a rather dramatic experience about which you will talk for a long time. You may draw pictures. You may look in the library for more books. You will certainly identify the alarm the next time it sounds and reminisce with your child about that special day. Your memory for the event, the books you have at home, and the toy firetrucks will probably stimulate enough of your child's memory for periodic conversations.

A colleague of mine, Dr. Pat Nilson, investigated the effect of enriched early experience on the speech and language competence of severely and profoundly hearing-impaired children. She discovered that the children who were more competent had more early life-enriched experiences with their mothers who were their primary caretakers.

Dr. Nilson found that the amount of formal speech and language therapy did not distinguish the more competent from the less competent children. However, she discovered there was a greater amount of **informal** parent therapy in the home, which characterized the more competent children as a group. Dr. Nilson learned that the parents of the more competent children did make extra efforts to provide a variety of experiences for their children in the form of trips into the community.

Some Ideas for Playful Productive Days

It may seem tiresome to think about organizing each day so that there are opportunities for language lessons and intellectual stimulation. However, this approach permits focusing your energy so that the opportunities to help your child are more easily available. The mothers of the more competent hearing-impaired children were distinguished by their motivation to make the most out of each experience. Using this basic idea, we may conclude that every event becomes a potential enrichment experience. Here are a few suggestions for your consideration, including how they might be elaborated. They may serve as preliminary suggestions that will enable you to create your own ideas.

A trip to the supermarket:

We all go marketing. Often it seems easier if we can leave our child home. Don't unless you must. There is so much to be experienced in the market that builds concepts, vocabulary, and competencies. In the supermarket you make choices and decisions. You can model these behaviors because you want your child to be good at choosing and deciding in many aspects of his life.

Every item has a name. Often you count the numbers of items you want to buy: e.g., 3 apples, 4 cans of juice. There is opportunity to learn about categories: e.g., fruit, vegetables, drinks, breads, etc. Then there are the individual members of each of these categories: e.g., members of the fruit groups include apples, pears, grapes, etc. Then there are subsets within the subset: e.g., varieties of apples include Macintosh, Delicious, Granny Smith, etc. Vegetables have different names, colors and shapes, all of which can be language labeled.

You may want to buy ice cream or other frozen foods which will involve planning. You do not want them to melt beforeyou get to the check out counter. When you choose the items you may carefully read the labels, beginning to introduce the idea of reading and written words. If you consider using visual symbols (see Chapter VII), you may want to give your child a list and help him be responsible for two or three items. There is much to do in the supermarket. It can be an important event. It is certainly one you must do for your family. It is a way of making good use of your own and your child's time.

A trip to the pizzeria for lunch (or to the ice cream store):

Who will go? Will you invite your child's playmate? Can your child make the invitation or does he need to observe you making it? How much will it cost? Gathering the money together introduces the idea of payment? How many pieces of pizza will you buy or what flavor ice cream? When you arrive who will get the napkins? Should we add some toppings? Will we buy a drink? Who will take responsibility for cleaning the table? After or before the event you can play the event out at home in an imaginary way or using real ice cream or pizza you have made together.

Going to a friend's birthday party:

You need to buy a present. What will your child's friend like? Going to the store to choose the gift is a project in itself. Choosing the paper and wrapping the present can keep you and your child busy, since it takes planning and measuring, cutting and taping. Will your child make a card? What will he wear? Who will be there? Will there be games? Can you prepare him for the games beforehand to ease his adaptation? Perhaps you will take pictures and begin to develop a scrapbook of important events. Looking at the scrapbook can be another way of remembering and talking about important experiences.

Inviting a friend to come over to play:

Social experiences are very important, even though your child may be so young that the play is likely to be more parallel than interactive. How will the invitation be made? By phone? In person? Your child will see you model the behavior and learn to do it someday himself. What time will the friend come? You can make a drawing of a clock and match it to the kitchen clock for the time of arrival? Will the friend come for lunch or a snack? Can you prepare it together? Where will they play? Indoors or outside? Who will clean up the toys?

Taking a walk around the neighborhood:

There is much to see and identify: dogs, cats, flowers, trees, etc. Maybe they can be counted. Perhaps you and your child can collect rocks or leaves on the way, step on the cracks on the sidewalk, smell the flowers, watch the workers build the new house on the block, talk to a neighbor, or make a new friend?

Watching the workmen pave the road:

There is a bulldozer and a dump truck set up on the road. There are men and one woman in hard hats. There is a lot of noise when they break up the old road. This could be an interesting event that permits development of new concepts and vocabulary in the real life situation that are difficult to teach in an abstract way.

Watching big kids play stick ball in the field:

Your child and you can see the game and how big kids relate. Then you can come home and play ball and have a "cooperative" game of your own, perhaps including some other little kids on the block.

Baking cookies or making popcorn:

Focus on the process not the product and you will have fun. You will need to "read" directions, measure, stir, mold, etc. You can have a party afterward or package the goodies to take to a friend or a neighbor .

The activities I have listed above are examples of opportunities to be together, to have fun, to share the experiences most of all, and to **talk**. Some experiences can result in unexpected events. I remember going with my two daughters to the Brooklyn Museum. They were not that interested in museums, and so we stayed a very short time. Outside we discovered a more wonderful "exhibit": an ant colony. We watched the busy ants carry bits of sand to build their ant hill for a much longer time than we spent in the museum. We talked about how hard the ants worked and how determined and committed they were to their hill building. This concept was far more interesting to them coming from the ants than any lecture with which I might have bored them!

Another time we stopped at a farm stand on the road to buy fruit and vegetables. Before long we made friends with the farmer's children who took us to the barn. There we climbed into the hayloft and into the silo. Tumbling down the silo was an unforgettable experience. Interesting events have frequently happened to us just because we went out into the world and **were open to the possibilities**.

Choosing Toys and Games: Vehicles for Conversation

In her study of hearing-impaired children Dr. Nilson also learned that the more competent hearing-impaired children in the development of speech and language had a great variety of toys. Some of the toys might have seemed too advanced for their chronological ages. For example, they had magnets, magnifying glasses, binoculars, microscopes, etc. These children could make use of these toys because playing was more frequently a shared experience with their parents. In the cooperative experience the children were helped to discover how to use more complex toys and manipulate them in a meaningful way.

For example, single-piece puzzles can be used independently by a toddler. However, manipulating a multi-piece puzzle with success is also possible but usually requires some assistance from an adult initially. The child should not be told where to put the pieces. He needs to be helped to learn how to approach the task and the process involved.

For example, the process involves learning to handle the parts inquisitively, conceptualizing the whole, and using multisensory clues including shape, color, and content. Exposing your child to this "discipline" is a kind of playful sharing between you and him. Sometimes a parent can offer this sharing by modeling or playing with the materials while talking aloud about what she is doing. This can take place beside your child who may actually be playing with another toy or a different puzzle. Sometimes you can share the process by doing a puzzle together, taking turns. The experience of constructing a whole from its parts is a very valuable experience for the hearing-impaired child. Your child need lots of this kind of experience to become really adept at building meaningful messages from auditory information that is usually limited.

It is also enriching to discover new ways to play with old toys. I am reminded of a rather expensive wooden form-board of circles, triangles and squares. There were four sizes of each shape. Each of the four was in one color. After Stephanie would empty the form-board and place the forms into their respective places, form-board play seemed to be over.

However, we discovered other possibilities: the colors could be stacked together; the largest shapes could be grouped; the increasing sizes could be sequenced for each form. Playing this way required that

I introduce new ideas and words like "sorting" the "same" characteristic such as "shape" or "color" and "comparing" sizes like "smallest" and "biggest."

Then we made a game. We put some of the shapes in a brown bag. As she got better at this game, we used more and more items. Stephanie would retrieve the one I requested by only using her tactile sense. I would describe the shape in words, "Give me the biggest circle." And if this was too hard I would add, "The biggest circle that fits into this space," pointing to the form-board. As you may anticipate this game once developed was expanded and I would be "it" too, receiving Stephanie's instructions. And the game did not stop at abstract forms. We would put objects of all sorts into the brown bags and exercise our tactile sense after the verbal challenge (or request) was made.

This play was focused on fun and success. I wanted Stephanie to have a challenge that would interest her and the success that would please her. This game which just occurred to me one day while we played together helped refine her perceptual-motor senses. Through the years we would set up thousand-and-more-piece puzzles on the dining room table and do them as a family. Stephanie was always the best at them. She is still a whiz at puzzles today. She uses them as an enjoyable and absorbing pastime and still sometimes mounts the finished product as we did when she was little.

There is the wonderful world of imaginary play which I have mentioned. It is enhanced when dolls, doctors kits, toy telephone, vehicles, blocks, kitchen center, etc. are available. Imaginary play permits your child to create a story and play it out. If your child will permit you into the play, you can help him elaborate his own ideas verbally or in action. As you respond you can program the appropriate language that fits the play. You can label actions and objects, develop concepts evolving from the play, and/or explore your own and your child's fantasy life.

For example, if your are getting ready to introduce toilet training, in a neutral way you can play out the toilet training with the dolls. Or, if you are want to teach about the importance and dangers of fire, you can bake in the toy oven, play out getting burned, and go to the doctor for care. You may even play out a make believe fire, calling the firefighters with toy horns, and playing out how to prevent a real fire from happening.

There are also many materials that can be used to foster creativity and expression. Plasticine, self-hardening clay, or play dough that you can make from flour, water, and food coloring are wonderful vehicles for using creative energy to construct images of the world. Making the play dough can be as much fun as playing with it.

Tempera, water color, and finger paints should be part of your household supplies. It is true these materials can make a mess. However, part of the fun is the "mess." Part of using the materials is learning to set up and clean up afterward. Part of the joy is creating a product that can be exhibited on the refrigerator or be given to a relative as a gift.

There are also musical instruments that can enrich experiences. Percussion instruments like drums, knockers, triangles, cymbals, etc. are good for developing rhythm. Stephanie and I would play a game in which one of us would create a rhythm with an instrument and the other would imitate it. This was a wonderful way to practice imitating the normal inflections of speech without feeling like it were a lesson.

Singing songs together is enhanced by the accompaniment of the "orchestra." Childhood songs like "Bingo," "My Hat It Has Three Corners," "Row, Row, Row Your Boat," "I've Got Six Pence," etc. are wonderful ways to share time together, learn language, develop rhythm, improve the resonance of the voice, and have a wonderful time together. The songs you do not know are available on children's records. You and your child can learn them and accompany them with the musical instruments. The instrument collection should include at least two kazoos. Whatever cannot be sung to satisfaction can be executed with great skill on a kazoo.

My favorite shopping was done in the toy store. There I found the materials around which much of my experiences with Stephanie developed. The toys were some of the vehicles for our creative pursuits and those playful times from which much of our communication evolved.

Organized Activities

The community in which you live may offer opportunities for structured activities for your child. There may be swimming for tots and infants, a gym program for tots, dancing lessons, art programs, music and movement programs, and play groups. The content of the activity is important. However, the social components of the experience are equally, if not more, important.

The more your child knows, the more confident he is apt to be. It is desirable to provide enrichment experiences for your child in an organized activity if the leader and your child can handle it. Observe a session and evaluate if your child has the capacity to participate at this time. Determine from your child if he is interested by giving him an opportunity to participate in a session. If you decide to enroll your child, help the instructor to learn how to communicate with your child by setting the model yourself and some simple encouragement.

Helping Others Learn to Interact with Your Hearing-Impaired Child

Your child will have teachers, leaders, and various helpers who will be ignorant about hearing impairments. They will have no notion of what to expect from your child. This is probably good. Your child and you can enlighten them. Other adults have stereotyped ideas that may interfere with their ability to interact productively with your child. Their biases may set limitations on their expectations and their involvement.

You want the best for your child from any teacher, leader, or helper who has the potential to enrich his life. Therefore, you want to dispel or reduce whatever anxiety the person may be feeling about interacting with your child.

Learn to be calm and free from intense anxiety yourself when you are intending to obtain help for your child. Anxiety is contagious. You do not want to give yours to anyone who will be helping your child. Learn how to use rhythmic and natural breathing to calm yourself. Try a yoga course or meditation if you need some formal instruction. Breathing oxygen is amazingly calming, better for you than any chemical tranquilizer. Learn to use it!

You do not want to make your child's needs bigger than they actually are. Keep your requests simple, straight forward, and brief.

Essentially you want the potential helper to understand that your child **hears with his ears and his eyes**. Suggest to the teacher-leader that if she can implement the following actions, she will be very helpful:

1. Face your child when she communicates with him.
2. Obtain his attention before she speaks.
3. Demonstrate a new behavior after she indicates her intention to show him something.
4. Indicate that another person is talking by pointing to him and calling him by name.
5. Encourage him to take a place in front and off center for the best perspective in the group.

Even better, you could neatly write these suggestions on a card or in a note after you conference with the teacher-leader. This written information could be a source of reference if needed. Whenever possible model these suggestions so that the teacher can see in your interactions with your child what works well.

Conclusion

Everything should be a topic for conversation between your and your child. While you can try to structure the interaction, it is desirable to follow the interest of your child. Talk about what he seems interested in. If you find your child does not engage you in his interests, then it is important that you try to engage him in what you think he might find interesting. Do not force more on your child when he seems to have had enough. Quit while you are ahead! If it is a good experience, your child will come back to it for more some other time.

Stay with the observable, concrete, and demonstrable. Use pictures when you cannot be in the actual experience. Move slowly from the tangible to the less tangible. It will be a while before you can talk of the abstract. A scrapbook and photo album would be very good investments of your efforts.

Whatever your child creates is wonderful. Both he and his productions should be admired with joy. The more you cherish him, the more he will cherish himself. This is the foundation that builds the self-esteem and self-confidence that he will always need.

It really does not matter what you and your child do together. What does matter though is that you are together sharing interesting experiences, enjoying one another, and discovering the world and each other. **This is what enriches your child and compensates for his hearing deprivation.**

Chapter VI

Learning to "Hear" What Cannot Be Heard

During those eventful days at the end of Stephanie's first year, I considered myself luckier than I had ever been. I would not have exchanged winning the million dollar lottery for the two timely events that determined the course of Stephanie's future. The first event was learning about Dr. Whetnall's work in England with hearing-impaired children who developed speech and language naturally and normally. I have discussed this in the Preface and in Chapter V.

The second event was meeting Dr. John Duffy. Neither of these people accepted hearing impairment as an automatically handicapping condition. They represented hope.

Dr. Duffy became Stephanie's audiologist and my mentor in those early years, when we were in pursuit of speech and language development. He was aware that there would be many hearing-impaired babies in the wake of the rubella epidemic of 1963 and 1964 of whom Stephanie was one. As Professor of Speech Pathology and Audiology at Brooklyn College of the City University of New York and Director of the Speech and Hearing Centers at Lenox Hill Hospital in New York and Kings County Hospital Center in Brooklyn, Dr. Duffy was very much involved in working with these children and their parents.

As we became acquainted, Dr. Duffy took the time to describe the method he would employ with the assistance of his speech therapists and myself to help Stephanie develop speech and language. He would continue to evaluate the hearing aids he had prescribed and determine that they were the best possible ones available for her. In addition to utilizing her remaining hearing to its fullest, he would follow a multi-sensory approach. He would also utilize the auditory, visual, kinesthetic, and motor avenues, giving Stephanie every means to develop her verbal language and speech.

However, there was a unique element in his program. When Stephanie had developed enough expressive language, he wanted to introduce the use of written words or visual verbal symbols to help improve the quality of her speech. She would be taught to associate familiar words, which she could hear and lip read, with written words.

In the early 1960's at the time of the rubella epidemic, Dr. Duffy had adopted the Initial Teaching Alphabet (ITA) of Sir James Pitman of England to spell the written words. Sir James had devised a 44-symbol alphabet (a phonetic alphabet) in which each letter symbol was assigned only one speech sound. This was a simplification of our traditional English alphabet of 26 letters in which many letters represent different sounds. A list of the ITA symbols and some illustrative words follow in Table 1. The additional eighteen symbols created by Sir James resembled traditional letters.

Table 1
Initial Teaching Alphabet

Symbol	Traditional Spelling	ITA Spelling
æ	plate	plæt
b	bed	bed
c	cat	cat
d	dog	dog
ee	feet	feet
f	full	full
g	leg	leg
h	hat	hat
ie	bite	biet
j	jug	jug
k	key	kee
l	letter	lettr
m	man	man
n	nest	nest
oe	toe	toe
p	pen	pen
ɼ	gi r l	gɼl
r	red	red
s	sat	sat
t	tree	tree
ue	use	ues
v	vat	vat
w	win	win
y	yes	yes
z	zebra	zeebra
ƨ	ea s y	ee ƨ ee
wh	when	when
ͨh	chin	ͨh in
ͭh	three	ͭh ree
ᴣh	the	ᴣh e
ʃh	shop	ʃh op
ᴣ	vision	vi ᴣ on
ŋ	rang	ra ŋ
ɑ	far	fɑr
aʊ	ball	baʊll
a	cap	cap
e	egg	egg
i	milk	milk
o	lot	lot
u	up	up
ω	book	bωk
⍵	spoon	sp⍵n
ou	out	out
oi	oil	oil

In practice, Stephanie would be taught to associate the written word spelled in ITA with the spoken word which she already knew. The sounds contained in the written words would then be isolated so that she would learn the individual speech sounds that comprised the word.

Dr. Duffy eventually provided me with examples as Stephanie's expressive vocabulary escalated. He explained that if she were to say " 'op" for "stop," it was because she heard the "o" and saw the "p." When she learned that "st" preceded the "op" by viewing the written word, she could be taught to include the "st." In a sense, she would be reminded of the "st" by the visual image of the written word. Eventually, her visual, kinesthetic, and motor memories of "stop" would remind her to say "stop" and not " 'op."

Dr. Duffy believed his method was a very effective means of improving articulation. His goal for Stephanie, while she was young, was to help her develop acceptable speech before poor speech habits became fixed. In addition this method could accelerate reading readiness and provide a solid foundation for learning to read which was an incidental and beneficial dividend.

Occasionally, I thought Stephanie's language and speech development was uncanny, almost as if she "heard" sounds through means other than her ears. I would learn much later as a graduate student that during the 1920's and 1930's there was a body of knowledge in experimental psychology that described sensory experiences in very broad terms. Hearing, for example, was enhanced through other sensory modalities. This helpful process was called synesthesia. For example, for some people the experience of listening to music is accompanied and enriched at times by visual experiences of color.

While I did not believe we had tiny auditory nerves in our skin, I did learn that the human being has a multi-sensory capacity to make sense out of the world one way or another. Hearing, according to this research, is not limited to the ears. This wholistic or multi-sensory notion of experiencing enhances the hearing-impaired child's capacity to comprehend the world.

In pursuit of the belief that language could develop naturally and normally, I was prepared to employ any ideas that made sense. If that meant believing in synesthesia, a sixth sense, early "reading," and ITA, I would pursue them.

Parents Are Active Participants

Dr. Duffy's ideas made sense. However, his ideas were not set forth in a system represented by an elaborate and tested program. It was a skeleton framework that provided concepts which he was elaborating with the help of his speech therapists. I would also have to make my own contributions to developing it. Dr. Duffy did not have recipes for me. He had some solid ideas, Pitman's alphabet, and Pitman's books. Furthermore, Pitman's books were not designed for babies. I had to create materials that would attract the interest of a baby. I suspect you can understand why I have stressed **creative** parenting in Chapter V. **We have to contribute actively to the systems that educate our children.**

Initial Procedures: The Way We Began

I do not believe I introduced any written words until Stephanie was eighteen months old. Dr. Duffy stressed that we could not start until Stephanie had enough expressive vocabulary. I remember feeling great anticipation and enthusiasm about this treatment without any real understanding about what I was getting myself into. I plunged in, planning for the big day when we could begin by first feeding Stephanie a rich diet of spoken words, sounds, and experiences. When she was eighteen months, we began to teach Stephanie written letters and whole words.

We did not wait have to wait until Stephanie was two years. Just as the theory indicated, the prophecy was fulfilled. Stephanie not only had a sizable receptive vocabulary by eighteen months, she also had a respectable expressive vocabulary as well. She was expresssing herself through speech which I have detailed in Chapter IV. "Dreams" were coming true. **Instead of focusing on her impairment, we were focusing on her growth.** We took off at eighteen months. Stephanie continued to use the ITA until she entered first grade and made the transition to our traditional alphabet.

Perhaps here is the time to confess that I was an exceptionally intense parent, as well as an exceptionally intense and active participant in the educational process. When the Director of the Queens College Early Childhood Center accepted Stephanie to their demonstration nursery school, I secretly thought she wanted to rescue

Stephanie from me! I was grateful that she wanted to provide an excellent early childhood experience for Stephanie. But I knew then that I was not just enriching Stephanie's experience. I was working in every possible way to compensate for her hearing impairment, because I did not know how much was enough. I gave my energy and all the bits of knowledge I was learning to Stephanie, because they were all I had to help her. I sometimes felt (and even now feel) like apologizing for my intensity. Yet I know that without it, she would have been lost to the silence of her very severe impairment.

We Played, We Labeled, We Learned

We did not start with individual sounds or symbols. The first approach was to enable Stephanie to associate the written word (visual verbal symbol) to objects which she could label with words. Since no one was directing me, I did whatever I thought was helpful. I was a free agent in a creative pursuit. Once Stephanie learned that the cards I made contained a form (a combination of letters or symbols) that was associated with an object, I began to label everything in our home. I was a big consumer of in posterboard, magic markers and masking tape.

There were labels on the doors, windows, tables, chairs, refrigerator, bathroom, bathtub, beds, etc. Everything was written in ITA which was easy enough for me to learn. However, most words we used were spelled with traditional spelling: e.g., car, dog, pin. Stephanie was able to discriminate the differences in the forms with relative ease. In part this was because I selected shapes that were easy to discriminate. For example, "door" looked very different from "refrigerator" which looked different from "tub."

There seemed to be another contributing factor to Stephanie's success with these written words. We had spent a lot of time doing puzzles, at which Stephanie was a whiz. Constructing a puzzle helped her develop skill in creating a whole from individual parts. Undoing a puzzle required that she separate the whole into its individaul parts. Having skill in moving in both directions seemed to make the learning of the visual verbal symbols relatively easy for Stephanie.

With the same creativity I used to interest her in playing so that I could expand her language, I developed games with the words. At first I chose words that had two, three, and four letters. These were very familiar to her, and easily distinguishable from one another. We would match them to the objects I collected, trying often to pick out some way of remembering the word. I would match words to objects just as she did. Eventually we used pictures along with the objects. I did not feel Stephanie was reading during these days. I did feel she was associating meaningfully to the visual-verbal symbols.

In research I conducted later with my colleague Dr. Nilson, we demonstrated that what Stephanie acccomplished was not unusual. Two year olds were quite capable of making these associations. We discovered that the two-year-olds with more enriched life experiences were better at it than their less sophisticated contemporaries.

In order to help Stephanie learn to more effectively discriminate among the words, I made use of every one of her senses. In this way she could compensate for what she did not hear. The initial "sound" of the word, as represented by the written symbol, was often the first focus of our attention. Initially we would outline it with our fingers. The "sound" was addressed by its sound quality or phonetic equivalent, not its alphabetical name. The "sh" in "shoo" (shoe) was "sh" not "s" "h." We would cross our lips with our index fingers and say "sh" as if to say, "Be quiet." This was like a cue.

Sometimes I would write a large symbol on a large piece of poster board. We would walk on the letter with our feet slowly or quickly, but always imprinting the sound into our muscles' memory. Sometimes we would try to imitate the letter with our bodies. This was not too hard to do for the "o" in "hot" or cooperatively with the "d" in "doll" or the "c" in "cry." Occasionally we would lie on the shape of the big letter on the posterboard which was fun if we were making a "t" as in "tooth" and had to lie on top of each other.

Sometimes, I would write the words with Stephanie. First, we would go to the store, choose colorful sheets of posterboard, decide on which two or three markers we would buy from the assortment of colors, and pay for the purchases. At home I would outline the symbols (letters) in pencil, and Stephanie would color them in. From this play she developed fine hand-eye coordination. She learned to handle scissors at an early age because we would cut out the letters together. We would match the new symbols to the old ones and to their respective objects. Other times, we would buy a new roll of tape, enjoy the pleasure of ripping off the wrapping, and then tape the newly outlined words to their proper place in our house. This required either matching the object with the original label or "reading" the new one.

As time went on, Stephanie's associative vocabulary increased. We would take down a bunch of words that hung from places in our home, mix them up, and then figure out where to put them back. It was a game: "Let's see where this one goes." As she became better able to identify the words, we would have scavenger-type hunts, where I would hide the objects for the words that were on our play table or I would hide the words for the objects in the most unlikely places. Then she would have to search for them and pair the object with the words or vice versa. When it was her turn to hide them, I would be "it" and she would check my "guesses." We played and Stephanie learned.

From these games Stephanie learned all the the 44 sounds in our speech system. There were many she could produce correctly. Some sounds were produced understandably, but not very well. Still other sounds were very much in need of speech therapy. Because I was not a speech therapist, I had a lot to learn from Stephanie's teachers who were employing the ITA symbols in the speech therapy. However, I felt that I was an important member of the helping team, since I had started the work of making sounds tangible in their written form which the speech therapist would teach.

Each sound had a symbol to identify it. Like Stephanie's other playthings these symbols had also become playthings. The sounds of language, whether heard or not, were real. Not one element of English speech was missing from Stephanie's auditory, visual, or kinesthetic repertoire. Once the speech therapy began, I became a student again, learning how to do it, too. Seated in the therapy room or observing through a one-way mirrored window, I would study how the therapist helped Stephanie learn to formulate the sounds causing her difficulty. These were usually the "s," "sh," and the "t" sounds and the blends like "st," "str," and the final "sts." At home I would reinforce the therapy from what I had learned.

Stephanie's second year was partly devoted to developing the tools to learn to say sounds correctly. This was so crucial because it was a way of interfering with the development of bad habits that result from saying words incorrectly. When this occurs, the habit patterns become so entrenched that it is extremely difficult to repair the speech errors. There is a long period of time that the child is too young to be watchful about correcting his own speech. Then there is a long period when the child is too resistant to correct his speech. Establishing as many correct speech patterns as early as possible saves a lot of anguish later on when there are more pressing developmental challenges facing the child.

Reading Books

I recall many parents who were pursuing different approaches to language enrichment and speech therapy. Many were dubious about my committment to Dr. Duffy's method. However, they were impressed with Stephanie's progress. Nevertheless, they raised their concerns about the possible confusion between the ITA and the traditional alphabet when Stephanie entered school.

I was not concerned about this. Therefore, when I read to Stephanie, usually at least once a day, I read from Pitman's little books written in ITA and children's books written in the regular alphabet. I was concerned only with the experiences the story could provide. The time to move from the phonetic ITA to the traditional alphabet was far away.

However, there was another consideration that freed me from the conflicts of other parents. I was not initially interested in teaching Stephanie to read. My energies were devoted to enabling her to hear sounds in whatever way was possible: through her ears, eyes, fingers, feet, skin, muscles, etc. Through these efforts I expected she would speak the words she was experiencing. I was willing to use any symbol system to accomplish these ends.

Fortunately, the ITA was sufficiently similar to our traditional alphabet. The visual-verbal symbols enabled Stephanie to speak more clearly. They also helped her learn to read in school with more ease than is common for severely hearing-impaired children. This early experience with letters and words probably helped her survive in the academic mainstream, as well.

The Simplified Phonetic Alphabet: An Alternative

Dr. Duffy has created an alphabet based upon the traditional English alphabet, the International Phonetic Alphabet, and the Pitman Initial Teaching Alphabet which resembles our traditional way of writing more than the ITA. He urges the use of this alphabet to provide a visual representation of spoken words for those hearing-impaired children who are capable of using it. Instead of the 44 symbols in the ITA, this phonetic alphabet has only 32 symbols, six more than our traditional alphabet. In the main, Dr. Duffy recommends its use in a manner similar to the ITA. However this alphabet requires fewer transitional adjustments, when the young child moves from this early tool to the more traditional reading material presented in school. You can review the symbols and compare the traditional and phonetic spelling in the list below, (Table 2).

In addition Dr. Duffy recommends cued speech to accompany spoken words as a means of helping severely hearing-impaired children develop verbal language and acceptable speech. Dr. R. Orin Cornett devised the original system of cued speech which is a visual supplement to normal speech. It consists of hand and finger cues presented very close to the face of the speaker. These visible cues represent the vowel and consonant sounds of normal speech. The cues enable the hearing-impaired child to use his vision to identify the speech sounds he cannot hear nor recognize visually. Unlike signing and finger spelling the cues do not substitute for speech.

As the hearing-impaired person or the normal hearing person speaks the finger configurations for each consonant and the hand position for each vowel accompanies each spoken syllable. This method can be used in its complete form or **selectively as needed.** The method of cued speech makes visual the sounds of language which might be otherwise inaudible or ambiguous. It is useful to the hearing-impaired person as a means of correcting speech and language patterns by observing others speaking during normal conversation or formal instruction.

Table 2
The Phonetic Alphabet of the
Modified Cued Speech Phonetic Alphabet Method

Symbol	Traditional Spelling	Phonetic Spelling
ɛ	beat	bɛt
i	bit	bit
æ	bait	bæt
e	bet	bet
a	bat	bat
u	but	but
ɑ	father	fɑther
o	hot	hot
ɔ	saw	sɔ
oe	go	goe
ω	book	bωk
⍵	blue	bl⍵
ai	eye	ai
oω	cow	coω
ɔi	boy	bɔi
r	river	rivr
y	you	yue
l	little	littl
w	we	wɛ
m	man	man
n	no	noe
ng	sing	sɛng
p	pat	pat
t	tell	tell
k	kiss	kiss
c	cat	cat
th	thin	thin
s	see	sɛ
sh	shoe	shω
ch	chat	chat
h	hot	hot
f	fan	fan
b	bat	bat
d	do	dω
g	go	goe
th	then	then
z	zoo	z⍵
zh	vision	vizhon
j	jar	iɑr
wh	when	when
v	van	van

Those who have used Dr. Cornett's method of cued speech have been enthusiastic about their success. Many professionals however, have avoided this method despite its promise, because it seems too complicated and difficult to learn. Over the past forty-three years as a professional involved with the hearing impaired Dr. Duffy has become convinced of the benefits of providing a visual system of cues to supplement the methods of teaching oral speech and language to hearing-impaired children. Impressed by Dr. Cornett's work and responsive to the criticism that the original system may have been too complicated, Dr. Duffy developed a modified version of Dr. Cornett's cued speech.

Dr. Duffy recommends that as many of the visual cues as needed be used in conjunction with oral speech and language stimulation and the use of phonetically spelled words. Therefore the child with more residual hearing and/or efficient lipreading skills would probably need fewer cues than a more severely hearing-impaired child.

Dr. Duffy's modified version simplifies the original cued speech of Dr. Cornett. Unlike Dr. Cornett's cues Dr. Duffy has included all vowels and semi-vowels within the four vowel hand positions. In the consonant groups each finger configuration has either unvoiced, voiced, or nasal consonants. What distinguishes Dr. Duffy's simplified modification is his separation of the unvoiced, voiced, and nasal consonants. In Dr. Cornett's system the unvoiced, voiced, and nasal consonants as well as the semi-vowels are dispersed throughout all eight-finger configurations.

Each position in Dr. Duffy's system represents vowels that look different on the lips. Finger configurations represent groups of consonants that appear visually different through lip reading. The written symbols of Dr. Duffy's new alphabet are associated with the cues. These cues become associated with the speech sound being perceived or produced. These cues do not represent word meanings like manual signs of American Sign Language or Signed English. **These cues only represent the sounds of speech**.

When I was first introduced to Dr. Duffy's new ideas, I felt somewhat overwhelmed. However, I remembered that I had developed a system of my own cues for Stephanie for certain sounds with which she had difficulty. For example, when I wanted to help her with the "st," "str," "sts," "s," "sh" and "t," I had created a simple way to model the tongue and lips with my hand. Essentially, I used cues to help her monitor her articulation. It was a simple system and helpful at the time. It occurred to me that Dr. Duffy and Dr. Cornett had formalized what I had informally developed to meet our needs. Thinking of cued speech from my personal experience made the new system less over-whelming. If I were in need of cues now, I would consider learning enough about Dr. Duffy's system to determine if it would be useful to Stephanie.

As I become familiar with this new method of cued speech and reconsider how much I needed to learn to help Stephanie, I recognize how difficult it is to learn new and technical procedures. **Patient, generous, and competent professionals are vital to our effectively helping our children.** In a sense every one of your child's teachers will be your teachers, as well. First, choose them carefully and then take all they are willing to give, but remember to **pay attention to your own opinions and contributions and to respect them.**

Learn As Much As You Can About Your Options: Sound Decision-making Depends on Informing Yourself

We have explored the importance of using every sensory avenue available to your child to help him acquire speech and language. We have looked specifically at some methods for making concrete or tangible sounds that cannot be heard through your child's ears or lipread through his eyes. These are approaches you may wish to consider for your child. You may not choose these options, but they may suggest other ideas to you that may suit you and your child better. The ITA was useful to Stephanie and me. There are other alphabets available if you decide to use the written word to supplement your child's early speech and language development.

In addition to the methods I have elaborated in this chapter there are other approaches that have been helpful to hearing-impaired children and their families that you may want to consider. For ex-ample, the auditory/unisensory approach is devoted to the development of oral speech and language. It stresses the use of the hearing-impaired child's residual hearing over the use of visual clues in order to strengthen the child's auditory functions. On the other hand, the Total Communication approach adds to the multi-sensory approach the use of signs and fingerspelling. For a more dtailed dis-cussion of Total Communication, please see Chapter III.

Among your many important decisions will be selecting the professionals who will teach you how to stimulate your child's language and speech. Before you can make this decision about which approach you will pursue and which teachers to choose, you will need to learn about the alternatives.

Our decisions are usually direct reflections of our values. In the next chapter we will be clarifying values. When you are more certain of what you believe, you will find it is easier to make these important decisions.

You Are the Keystone

Whatever you decide for your child will affect you as well. The teachers you choose will teach both of you. But you, the parent, will have to carry out the program you have chosen and teach the important parts of it to everyone else involved with your child. The simpler the program is, the less involvement is required of you. The more the program encompasses, the more you may need to invest. There is usually a relationship between the investment and the dividends. The more you put in, the more you are likely to benefit. In the case of your hearing-impaired child, the investment is energy, the risk is minimal, and the benefits are, at the very least, **the gift of communication and a chance at a balanced life that can result.**

Chapter VII

The Mentally Healthy Self

Although I was eager to become a parent, I felt fairly unprepared for my baby's arrival. I had a younger sibling for whom my parents wanted me to be responsible, but I was uncooperative. I did study child development in college, but felt mostly frustration at being expected to memorize developmental hurdles from birth. The parents preparation course I took at the Visiting Nurses Association taught me how to wash a doll. The most significant preparation I probably obtained was from being a babysitter, a camp counselor, and a third grade teacher. In each job I was interacting with real little people in some position of responsibility.

These limited experiences, however, did not reassure me in those terrifying early days of Stephanie's infancy, when I did not know what to do and I realized that she was totally dependent on me. For most of us it is usually not until we are on the parental line of responsibility that we really learn what parenting is about. Then we often reassure ourselves that if we survive the first child or if our first child survives in spite of us, we could have a second or third child to correct the inevitable mistakes.

In order to survive in the parenting business, we usually parent overtly or covertly in the manner in which we were parented. Some of us think this is fine because we feel okay about how we turned out. Others of us tend to feel "messed up" by our parents and take an oath to behave differently. However, there is a very strong likelihood that the parents we have internalized will take over automatically because their influence has left some very profound memory traces in us. Furthermore, when we are faced with the need to make important decisions quickly, it is easier to respond with the most familiar behavior, and it is probably one of our parent's behaviors that we repeat. Whether we like it or not, the most important teachers of parenting we have are our own parents who are inside us.

If we disavow the value of our parents' input because of what we feel were their mistakes, we are critical of ourselves, as well. This is not too good for our own self-esteem. We need every bit of good feeling about ourselves to parent our child effectively. On the other hand, to adopt our parents ways indiscriminantly without consideration for our child's being another different individual is to approach the parenting process from a narrowed perspective.

Values Clarification: How to Avoid Automatically Repeating Our Own Parents' Behaviors

There is a strategy that can be effectivly employed to tackle the problem of automatically behaving like our own parents without first reflecting about what we actually feel or believe. The strategy is called VALUES CLARIFICATION. The strategy is based upon a very simple concept: our behavior is an expression of how we think and feel. Sometimes we behave in ways that seem in conflict with what we feel or think. This can be disconcerting because most people derive a sense of confidence and comfort from believing that their thoughts, feelings, and behavior are in harmony.

To begin to clarify our values regarding child rearing, it is necessary to think out how we feel about life's possibilities. We can eliminate our automatic, indiscriminate responses by introducing reasons into the child-rearing process. This involves a self-imposed behavior modification plan based upon forethought and common sense.

I would like to introduce some ideas that you may want to consider as potential values to guide your behavior in relation to your hearing-impaired child, not only because they may help you but because they may be in your child's best interest. You may find yourself already in sympathy with these fundamental values, or they may be a relatively new set of ideas for you. In each case I will clarify the psychological impact on your child to help you to decide if the ideas are of value to you as a parent.

The Art of Giving: A Very Delicate Balance

The following sketches illustrate how the act of giving can create problems. Each person described below instructs us about the delicate balance in giving help, support, and our emotional presence to our children.

Laurie is desperately trying to develop a career. She came to me because she was being harassed on her job. She manages men on an assembly line. The men do not like her authority and how she delivers it. They resent when she enforces the "rules". She recently had three flattened tires and discovered a snake in her locker. The union is filing countersuits against her in response to her disciplinary actions against some of the men. She is furious with the men and afraid of them as well. To further complicate her life, she is on probation in college where she is pursuing her bachelor's degree She will be dropped unless she passes her course with an "A." She cries because she cannot imagine how she will write her term paper.

Laurie tells me that she never wrote her own compositions in elementary school or term papers in high school. Her mother would review her first drafts and then send her off while mother re-wrote the work. She is feeling helpless and resentful because of her sense of impotence and her lack of experience to cope with the current challenges in college and on the job.

The relationship in her life that is filled with the greatest interpersonal problems is the one with her mother. She can see that with all good intentions her mother took over most of her life. Laurie deferred to her mother to the point of becoming impotent. In her supervisory work she becomes her mother, takes over, and treats the grown men as infants. She alienates her subordinates by expecting them to be irresponsible and inadequate. She believes her mother treats her as if she were inadequate. She defers to her mother's authority. She cannot understand why the men do not defer to hers.

Sixteen-year-old Karen thinks she hates her mother. Her single mother has finally found a wonderful boyfriend after ten years of loneliness. Mother is invested in this new relationship and acknowledges to Karen that she has shifted her attention away from her. Previously, mother did everything for Karen who was her main companion. Without any preparation Karen must now do everything by herself that was done for her: cook her own dinners, do her own laundry, check her own homework, spend the weekends alone, etc. Mother who was always present is gone. Karen feels abandoned. She is furious, paralyzed, belligerent and oppositional.

Danielle's parents came to see me. Father is a businessman and mother is a homemaker. Danielle is failing all her subjects in her senior year of high school. Last year while a junior in high school her parents arranged a system of checks, where each teacher reported to them every Friday on Danielle's weekly performance. She managed to pass her courses with grades of "C" and "D."

The parents are exhausted and realize they cannot enlist her high school teachers in this policing and infantilizing project. They are embarrassed, but also angry over Danielle's impotence and dependency. Father remarks that Danielle is his baby. He is profoundly struck by his next thought -- she behaves like one.

I learn from Danielle that while she appreciates her parents love, she cannot stand their constant punishments, when she gets progress notes of unsatisfactory performance from school. However, she acknowledges that she feels stupid and worries that she is not smart enough to pass her courses. She has come to understand that her parents are acting like she is not smart enough and cannot pass without their help. She is confused. She is also guilt-ridden about her parents. They are so good to her. Why does she feel so angry with them?

These young women have come with problems that are not easily solved and more complex than these brief descriptions can adequately convey. In each case, however, the condition reflects some problem in what their parents have "given." The parents were well-intentioned, but something went wrong.

Each person I have very briefly described has been intruded upon in some way. They have been deprived of the opportunity to fulfill their own potential and experience a sense of self-worth. Each young woman now feels inadequate and dependent. Defeat threatens one, conflict and rage affects the second, and confusion plagues the third. There are many reasons for the difficulties experienced in each situation. But in all of them there seems to be confusion in the parental giving behavior: giving care, giving support, and giving an opportunity for self-sufficiency.

This issue of giving is particularly important to us as parents of hearing-impaired children. In addition to having all the usual problems of growing up, our children also have the additional problem of coping with a physical disability. Not only have we the task of nurturing a child to a mentally healthful adulthood, but we have to grapple with the effects of our child's physical condition.

How to Avoid Spoiling Your Child

By considering some of the dilemmas we may encounter in giving to our children, we may be able to clarify this value. As a general rule, every time we do something to or for our child that he can do himself, we are probably giving unnecessarily and unwisely. In a sense we are spoiling it for him. This is a fundamental definition of "spoiling." Situations of this sort run the gamut from anticipating a need not yet felt by our child, trying to facilitate completion of a task going steadily at our child's best pace, correcting a condition that is satisfactory and may not need correction, and assuaging unhappiness that is tolerable when we would be wiser to let the child cope with it independently.

Let Him Develop His Own Competence Independently

The events that can lead to our spoiling "it" for our children occur every day throughout the day. Giving a feeding before the baby has communicated hunger may result in interfering with the development of an important communication skill. Giving a new toy and immediately demonstrating how it should be played with may deprive the child of an opportunity to explore and discover the varied experiences the toy offers. Correcting a child's play or verbal response when his efforts are "good enough" communicates that you feel his production is inadequate. Interfering and settling a non-destructive sibling conflict or a neighborhood spat deprives the children of learning to settle conflicts independently. Demonstrating that you can perform your child's task without being asked for help exercises **your** competencies. However, taking over deprives your child of discovering and practicing **his own** skills that will contribute to **his own** sense of competence.

Certain parental behaviors infantilize rather than support the developing competencies and power in the child. Examples of this include dressing your child in part or completely, when he can do it himself; feeding your child, what he can feed himself; cleaning up **for** your child, rather than **with** him; speaking for your child what he can say for himself.

When people interact with a disabled person whom they perceive as handicapped, there is a tendency to give more than they might give to a "normal" person. Have you noticed how we tend to speak for the one who stammers, "reach" for the one who is limited, and "perform" for the one who is incapacitated. We are inclined to think of ourselves as selfish, if we do not do for someone what he has difficulty doing for himself.

Sometimes it is just too anxiety-provoking to stand by while someone struggles to do what we can help them with easily. Occasionally we may even feel the discomforting relief that we are whole and thus try by helping the person to ward off a similar mishap to ourselves. Some of us have a need to rescue a person in difficulty and thereby obtain love or derive a sense of power.

The Art of Giving: Not Too Much, Not Too Little

Whatever our motives are, we may actually do more harm than good by giving help inappropriately. For example, by helping unnecessarily we may interfere with the expression of the person's capability and his sense of competence. Or, we may communicate our sense of his inadequacy or lack of faith in his ability or his potential, surpressing or discouraging his motivation to be competent. In our do-good efforts we may deprive him of the opportunity to try himself and experience a self-fulfilling success; emasculate him with the attitude that we lack faith in his ability to succeed; or discourage him from taking the initiative and tackling the challenges.

On the other hand, we may err at the other extreme by giving too little. For example, we may push too hard before the person is ready with skills and confidence to perform a task. Or, we may set goals or expectations too far beyond his ability. Under these circumstances, he is destined to fail or become extremely frustrated if he tries, because the task is too overwhelming. At these times we may be judgmental, hostile, and punitive.

Knowing just how much pressure to apply and how much support to give is a difficult task. This is the parental challenge in the art of giving. If the balance is right, our child can to fulfill his potential, enjoy a sense of competence, and experience mastery. Self-esteem is built, self-confidence is felt, and energy is released to address the next challenge.

It is difficult to know how far we should move into our child's immediate personal space with support and encouragement. In part we can judge by experiencing our child's response. If our child is trying and immersed in his efforts, there is no need to interfere. If our child begins to err, this is not an indication to mobilize to help. The error can be instructive, and the child may learn something to guide him to another maneouvre. Trial and error efforts are a kind of experimental behavior. They should be nurtured and applauded, because it is a problem-solving skill that will be useful again when the obvious answer is unavailable.

It is at the point that your child looks for help that you need to make a decision to act. At this point you may want to encourage another try, give a hint, or lend a hand. But you do not want to take the experience away and selfishly deprive your child of the opportunity to grow.

It is not uncommon, when your child reaches a stumbling block, for him to look to you for the rescue. Frequently this occurs if you have conditioned him to expect to be rescued. In fact, under these pre-established conditions, your child has learned that at the sign of his frustration you will take over. Parents often blame their children for manipulating them into taking over. **They fail to recognize the "manipulative" behavior was taught long before by the parents themselves who ran to the rescue every time there was some frustration.** As this child gets older, the parent becomes disappointed in his child's dependency, experiences some degree of anger, and wishes to withdraw leaving the child to his own plight. The child often feels the threatened abandonment, becomes panic-stricken, and clings in greater dependency and impotence.

The child who pigheadedly must do everything himself presents a different problem. This child rejects support and struggles for control. Extreme independence may deprive this child of benefiting from external input. It is undesirable that the hearing-impaired child develop attitudes that place him at the extremes of accepting help: i.e., overdependence that borders on helplessness or extreme independence that borders on inappropriate grandiosity. Ideally the hearing-impaired child should be helped to learn to function to the best of his ability in a cooperative interpersonal manner and be willing to take assistance from others that will help him become self-fulfilled.

Two Questions That May Help You Find A Happy Medium

It is difficult to write prescriptions on the delicate balance in the art of giving. Determining the right dose of giving is a feat of human sensitivity. You are more likely to give an appropriate dose if you value your child's development of mastery and competence. There are two questions you might raise for yourself as your think about the balance:

(1) How far should you move into your child's **physical** space to provide tangible and direct "help"?

(2) How far should you enter into his **emotional** space with the more intangible supports of your encouragement and trust in his abilities?

Sometimes the right degree is attained by simply being close by. The appropriate degree is rarely delivered by standing on your child's toes or intruding into his shoes. Respect for his boundaries may be a guide to just how far is "too far."

Where Will Control Be Located: Inside or Outside?

When our hearing-impaired children are born they are innocent victims of some unfortunate event: a genetic accident, an *in utero* infection or illness, a constitutional birth defect, etc. Even if their impairment is post natal caused by an early childhood illness, they are still innocent victims of events over which they have had no control. As their parents we share their victimization. We may despair and be embittered. Like our children, we too will be marked indelibly by this event.

It is a generally accepted fact that what happens to us early in life has a profound affect on our later development. Living one's life feeling like a victim is not conducive to a healthy adjustment and a viable sense of personal control. Yet it is certainly reasonable that our children might come to feel victimized and powerless, if the condition of their disability results in their believing they have limited opportunities.

When it comes to notions of a personal sense of control, psychologists sometimes divide people into two groups based on general attitude: (1) people who believe things "happen" to them, and (2) people who believe they "can make" things happen. Psychologists have labels for these attitudes. The people who feel they are victims of circumstances are said to have an "external locus of control" because they turn control over to external sources. Those who feel they have a controlling impact on the events occurring in their lives may be said to have an "internal locus of control."

We are inclined to develop a predominantly internal or external locus of control orientation based upon our life's experiences. If we have had frequent opportunities to notice that we are responsible for events, our internal locus tends to be reinforced. If we notice that nothing we do seems to make a difference in how things turn out for us, we tend to feel impotent and surrender control to more powerful external sources. These orientations evolve over the course of our life's experiences.

Our hearing-impaired children are very dependent on reinforcement and feedback in the development of their locus of control. The more experiences they have that will reinforce their sense of internal control the more likely that their early sense of victimization will be altered. This will affect and increase their belief in their own power and potential.

A healthy sense of self emanates from feelings of self-respect, self-sufficiency, self-confidence, and self-fulfillment. These feelings more easily develop from a predominantly internal or self-directed locus of control. It is fairly evident that encouraging the development of an internal locus of control in our children is desirable, if they are to realize their full potential. So while we may painfully acknowledge the powerful effect of their early deprivation and victimization, we can be encouraged by the ameliorative maturing potential of experiences that will contribute to a sense of personal control.

Now that the concepts are defined, it is important to clarify that life's events are neither all externally or internally controlled. Consider environmental forces. There are natural conditions like hurricanes and blizzards that we cannot control, though we can prepare for them. There are also external human conditions over which we as individuals can have minimal effect except for group membership or the vote: e.g., decisions we oppose made by goverment officials, corporate presidents, or insane dictators.

Then there are some events that are partially outside and partially within our control. Usually these are the events that affect our personal lives directly. For example, we cannot prevent a person from attempting to burglarize our home if he chooses. However, we can secure our homes from attempted burglaries through any number of strategies: e.g., by installing a special alarm system, informing the police of our absence, getting a house sitter, keeping five Doberman pinschers, etc.

There are events that are very much within our control. Given the educational system provided us, we have extensive opportunities to choose how to educate ourselves for an occupation so that we have employment opportunities and financial security. We can choose to extend our longevity by eating wisely and exercising to keep our bodies in good health. **And** in the same way we can take over and actively parent our hearing-impaired children. They will become competent in their development of speech and language skills but also, and **just as important, they will become sufficiently mentally healthy to handle their life's challenges.**

How to Foster an Internal Locus of Control: Sharing Decision-Making and Problem-Solving

If fostering the development of an internal locus of control seems of value to you, then you will probably decide to treat your child as if he does have control over aspects of his life. This requires that early in his life you will give him opportunities to make decisions and execute them. It means sharing your parental authority over him **with** him. This does not mean a two-year-old is in control of his daily living to the point that he might engage in potentially hurtful behavior. However, it means that whenever possible you and your child share the responsibility of: (1) Thinking about a problem (challenge, situation, decision, "opportunity," etc.) which has been as clearly defined as possible, (2) Generating potential solutions to solve the problem, (3) Choosing from among the options or solutions a course of action, (4) Executing the chosen solution, and (5) Evaluating final choices to determine if the problem is satisfactorily solved.

The sense of internal control starts with your attitude which conveys the belief that your child is capable of learning to make wise decisions. It is facilitated by providing opportunities at his level of maturity which give him a chance to make wise decisions. These require a balance between "giving" guidance and support and restraining your parental "take-over" mechanism.

For example, you will probably be talking a fair amount about the food you give your child to eat. Once your young child can discriminate between milk and juice, an early decision-making experience is encouraging him to decide when he wants a drink which it will be. Weather and clothing will undoubtedly be a topic of conversation in the "language lessons." As the language and concepts are learned, your child may be able to help you decide upon the appropriate jacket, pants, or footwear when it is time to get dressed and go outdoors.

As his language and speech develop and he matures, he will be ready for bigger decisions. For example, you will have many occasions to demonstrate the appropriate way to cross the street. You can talk for many years about the considerations that enter the decision. In the course of these discussions before crossing you may encourage him to participate in the decision making as a partner with you. In time he may be ready to take your hand and help **you** to cross.

If you have done well, he will probably help you cross the street in much the same way you have been helping him. This investment of your effort will eventually be followed by your child crossing streets entirely on his own. For the sake of your nerves, it pays to start this training from the first streets he crosses with you.

As your child continues to grow it will be important for you to teach him the value of his time and the importance of budgeting it wisely. He can be expected with this kind of values training to decide when to do his homework and how much time to devote to it. He can be helped to learn that television watching is an activity that should be time limited. Deciding how to spend that time by choosing programs wisely can grow from this valuing of time. This early exposure will affect how your child thinks about his leisure-time experiences.

These types of decisions could affect the choice of his companions. Being accepted by his peer group is complicated by his being different. For most kids it is not a simple matter of choosing whom he wants for friends. It involves finding those who want him as well. Add to this the possibility of his being confronted with the peer pressure to buy drugs, smoke cigarettes, or drink alcohol. Then he will be required to utilize his sense of personal control and his decision-making skills for some rather critical problem-solving.

By investing early in your child's ability to manage his life effectively, it will make your life easier in two major ways. First, you will not have to parent twenty-four hours a day. You will be free to have a portion of your own life separate from parenting. Secondly, you will have the peace of mind that comes when you have faith in your child to take intelligent care of himself.

The payoff for your child is monumental. By effectively tackling his decisions he builds self-confidence and self-esteem. He receives your respect. He demonstrates to himself that he is in control of his own existence and capable of managing his own affairs.

I am reminded how actively involved my husband and I were with Stephanie when she was applying to college four years ago. In contrast, she handled her graduate school applications and interviews independently, offering a piece of information to us every now and then. She managed to get herself admitted to several graduate programs, including her first choice.

I am impressed by her independence and resourcefulness which reassures me (and probably her as well) that she is very likely to successfully handle a difficult graduate program and the demands of a human service profession. This achievement is, at least in part, the partial product of our nurturing an internal locus of control, which has yielded a very large return on our investment. We still nurture the internal locus of control. And we still provide support and help when it is needed. You will discover that you will not become expendable. On the contrary, you will simply be asked for appropriate assistance, at each age.

The Value of Appreciating the Psychological Impact of the Hearing-Impairment on Your Child

The feeling of being a victim is intertwined with the loss of hearing. Suffering such a profound loss so early in life inevitably results in a very significant impact on personality development. If the impairment is congenital or happens immediately, the loss is a fact of birth. Your baby does not have the experience of once having had something that is then lost. Instead, he learns as he matures that he has lost something he has never experienced or experienced only very briefly.

The Sense of Loss and What It Means

In a sense, your child begins to learn of his loss as his family discovers it and communicates this knowledge to him. They learn something is wrong. The child begins to learn he is missing or lacking something very important. He learns that people dear to him are very unhappy that he cannot hear normally. He may begin to think he has done something wrong to earn this condition. He could begin to think he is bad. He may even start feeling guilty. It takes time for the hearing-impaired child to integrate these ideas. However, the fundamental pieces of information are operating in a fantasy of the child's own making. Unfortunately, it generally has a negative impact on his personality development. For each child the fantasy is a personal narrative or explanation regarding what has happened to him. In each case, however, there is at least one similarity: very early in life something very important was lost.

Loss is often one of the hallmarks of depression. First our children experience very early in life a physiological loss. Then they experience the psychological components of the loss with which they will live through their entire lives.

This business of loss is a very important part of personality development. Each of us suffers experiences of loss throughout our lives. The impact of loss is important to understand so that we will better appreciate our children's experience as well as our own. First, consider loss as it affects most people regardless of their capacity to hear normally. Each of us started out very early, at birth in fact, having lost our original position in the womb. There we did nothing but exist, being nurtured effortlessly with whatever we needed. It was a perfect place in a primarily stressless relationship.

Although infancy is not usually a demanding period of life, we did have to learn to put up with the loss of immediate gratification. For example, we could be kept waiting for our food, the temperature could turn cold if we lost our blanket, we might suffer gastro-intestinal discomfort, or we might be roughly handled, ect. None of these unpleasant conditions were present in the womb.

While the first loss occurs for all of us whether hearing or hearing impaired at birth, other losses soon follow during our first year. We may not have the exclusive attention of the person caring for us and have to share attention with other family members. We have to learn that our caretaker is not attached to us but is actually a separate person. Once we come to grips with this separateness, then we can no longer hold on to notions of our power. We have to give up the idea that all we need to do is wish for a feeding or a dry diaper and by magic we can make it happen. This fantasy is possible, because as infants we live in a fused state or union with the people responsible for us. It is an achievement of infancy which heralds developing individuality, when we recognize our caretaker to be separate. This recognition represents a change or loss in our original notions about how the world works.

Then all of us experience some real life painful losses: e.g., the loss of maternal attention with the arrival of a younger sibling or the diversion of parental attention to an older sibling. This loss of exclusive attention is rather disconcerting. The girls in my nine-and-ten year-old therapy group compete continuously for my attention. They help me understand how important my exclusive attention is to them. With increasing age and understanding the losses are easier to understand though not necessary easier to accept. For example, the family cat or dog may die. A familiar and often available grandparent may become ill and go into the hospital, resulting in a loss of their presence and attention. The grandparent might become very ill and die, which would represent the final loss through death.

All this can be very hard to understand and for some of us difficult to accept. Loss through death can have profound effects in the scheme of personality development. I treat a bright little boy who witnessed the slow and tragic deterioration of his mother from a brain tumor. This continued for a period of three years and culminated in four months of his witnessing her vegetative existence. He is not able to focus too long on the experience of his loss. However, when I explore with my pre-adolescent and adolescent patients who have lost a parent through death early in their lives, their words express for them (and for this little boy) how profound the loss was.

It is crucial therefore, that we understand by use of these comparisons that many of our hearing-impaired children suffer an early profound loss. Their's is initially a loss of sensory functioning caused by a physical impairment. This loss will be re-experienced at least unconsciously with every other loss and threat of impairment that follows in their lives. This is a psychological condition. It is very sad. It need not interfere with functioning nor make for excuses. It may even have positive consequences in the pursuit of self-fulfillment. Yet this condition should be respected as a significant influence that contributes to personality development.

I suspect there are hearing-impaired people who have not experienced the sense of loss I have described. These people have probably been hearing-impaired since infancy and have lived in predominantly or exclusively deaf communities with their family members who are also deaf. Sign language is their means of communication. Absence of hearing is probably perceived as a condition of their lives. It is possible they do not consciously miss the hearing they never had.

I am reminded of a hearing-impaired woman who was very much in the mainstream. She came to see me because her hearing-impaired husband wanted a divorce. She went into a debilitating depression. Her job performance was affected badly. She was placed on probation by her job supervisor which intensified her depression. This divorce represented a profound loss of a loved one, a companion, and a life style. It was symbolically related to all the other painful losses in her life. When her grandfather and father became ill subsequently, she had rather extreme but understandable anxiety responses that each would die. She experienced the selling of her house as a loss which was also very painful for her.

I could not change a single one of these painful reactions, though she wished I had some magic. What she could get from me was the willingness to try to **help** her **help** me understand. Fortunately, she had the words and the motivation to discover new words for feelings she had not previously acknowedged. This experience of self-understanding became a source of pride, as she gained increased understanding of the reasons for her distress. She felt better simply knowing that she was no longer a victim of painful, mysterious feelings.

This emotional understanding conveyed through your eyes, body, words, and spirit is what your child will need from you. You may need this understanding from others, since you too have suffered a loss. "Simply being understood" tends to free the preoccupation with the problem and then frees the formerly preoccupied energy for more adaptive pursuits.

In addition to being depressed, your child will be and feel different. However, he will not only be different because of the combination of his genetic makeup and the influence of environmental experiences on his life as is the case with most other people. He will also be different from the majority of people who hear normally and speak with relative ease. This difference automatically puts him into a minority group with which he will have to reckon eventually. Being different is not easy throughout childhood, but especially difficult during pre-adolescence and adolescence. We will discuss the challenges of these developmental periods in Chapter IX.

Before we move into the developmental periods, however, we will consider in Chapter VIII what are the special conditions that being hearing impaired imposes on our child's life. It is important that we do not lose sight of the fact that our children are indeed "special" and deserve some very "special" treatment.

Chapter VIII

Who Am I
and Where Do I Belong?

As I work in my study I hear Stephanie phoning one of her friends without using the TDD. The TDD (telecommunication device for the deaf) is a telecommunications machine that includes a typewriter key board and flashes the written words on a screen. Conversation is written not spoken. I hear her ask, "Is Wendy home?" I am drawn to her door, conflicted about offering help she has not requested.

Lately, her sister, father and I have been so busy that we have been inconvenienced by her need for us to be her telephone interpreters. She has become accustomed to our reluctance and fights back with anger. She does not like her dependence. She would like to give every one of her normal hearing friends a TDD. Recently, she has preferred not to ask us for help. Instead she has taken to making phone calls herself. As I stand with my hand on the doorknob, I am full of remorse for my irritation and reluctance.

Through the door I hear Stephanie say, "When will she be home?" The person responds. I sense she cannot understand. I turn the knob and intrude. I ask if I can help. She seems appreciative and yet irritated by my appearance. She asks the person again and turns the amplified receiver toward me. I listen. The person speaks with a very thick accent. I can barely understand him. He understands Stephanie. I gather Wendy is not there. I interpret that he says she should call tomorrow. Stephanie thanks him and hangs up. I have an overwhelming feeling of sadness.

I reassure Stephanie that he was very difficult to understand. She explains he is Wendy's grandfather who has a very thick Greek accent and great difficulty with English. I feel a flood of mixed emotions including awe, admiration, and confusion. How could she be so unrealistic as to try to hear on the phone with her very severe impairment? I am distressed, wondering if she really accepts her severe hearing impairment. I discount the ridiculous thought. Of course she does. But, she does not act like this hearing impairment is part of her.

Finally she makes one of her rare confesssions about her hearing impairment. The greatest frustration from her hearing impairment is her inablitiy to use the telephone. This limitation has seriously interfered with her social life. She is enraged!

As I shared this brief moment with her, Stephanie put her struggle with who she is and where she belongs into some perspective for me. The telephone is a symbol, like her hearing aids, of how she is different. Her impaired hearing separates her socially because she cannot use the phone like everyone else. On this day I can see how determined she is to overcome its interference in her life.

Of late Stephanie does not always use the TDD in phone conversations with me. In the past year she has learned to use the rhythm of word combinations, the inflections in sentences, the meager sounds she hears, and environmental events to "figure out" my messages. She has no problem communicating hers. At the end of these strictly oral telephone conversations, I know if we have been able to communicate, when she repeats back to me accurately what she thinks I am saying. She knows we have succeeded when she hears "yes" or "no" from me. She can distinguish these two words on the phone with relative ease. At these moments I get a mystical feeling and attribute the event to magic, synesthesia which I discussed in Chapter VII, and her ability to use every bit of her resources. Stephanie's achievement seems incredible, since she hears very little.

I am awed by Stephanie's unwillingness to accept her limitation. I admire her courage. I respect her efforts and determination. I feel pride with her when she is successful. But I am confused because I cannot explain her success rationally. I am sad for her. However, I consider her fortunate that she is motivated to grow through this problem and overcome her limitation. Her impairment is a part of her identity, even if sometimes she tries to minimize it, like struggling on the phone. However, she has reached a point in her life where she no longer wants her impairment to alienate her from others or restrict her choices of where she fits in.

Early Decisions Cast a Lasting Imprint

For years after Stephanie left nursery school, I wondered if she might have been happier in a school for the deaf. There she would have known many more people with hearing impairments and have been less different from her peers. However, my needs, goals, and attitudes led to decisions about her education.

These decisions have contributed to the person she perceives herself to be today. I treated her as if she could hear a great deal more than her audiogram indicated. As a result she learned to "hear" far beyond the limits of her very severe impairment. She treats herself today like a person who can use the phone without the TDD. She has confided that she uses the phone this way to give messages and to receive pre-arranged or very limited messages. This is not a small achievement. The fascinating thing for all of us is that she can successfully understand the message!

As we move through this chapter, we will explore the first seeds you will be planting of your child's sense of self and where he belongs. We will consider the decisions with which you will be confronted and the direction you will give to your child's sense of who he is, his education and his social experiences. These will significantly affect his identity and what challenges you and he may face in the future.

Examining Some of the Possibilities: Some Hearing-Impaired Young People

I have known some hearing-impaired young people in different capacities--as a psychologist doing research, as a clinician providing therapy or evaluation, and as the mother of their friend. The people to whom I would like to introduce you have made different adjustments. I have disguised them and used different names to protect their privacy. These descriptions will give you an idea of some of the possible ways hearing-impaired young people can grow up.

I have known Diane since she was four years old. She has a mild to moderate impairment in one ear and a very severe impairment in her other ear. With the use of her hearing aid in her better ear, she hears within the hard-of-hearing range. Diane is a pretty, well-groomed, attractive, and engaging twenty-year-old. She is articulate. There are minimal speech and voice clues that would indicate she is hearing impaired. She can talk on the phone using her good ear. She is completing college at a university for normal hearing students and plans to go on to graduate school. While she has many hearing-impaired friends, she lives predominantly within the normal hearing community.

Diane is a traveler. At her university she has made friends with many foreign students. She has traveled around the world during her three years in school--sometimes en route to visit a college chum home on vacation and sometimes to a foreign country with or without a traveling companion.

When Diane was in high school, she was very active in extra-curricular activities. She played first-string girls basketball. Her hearing problem did not interfere with her ability to communicate with her teammates. Her competitiveness won her team big points.

Anthony is a profoundly hearing-impaired man in his late twenties, whom I have known since his early childhood. I had the privilege of testing his intelligence when I was a graduate student. I did not have to score the results to know he was of very superior ability. He practically scored the test for me, indicating what should come next and exploring my manual inquisitively to make sense of it.

His audiogram indicates that he has limited residual hearing. It is notable that he did not receive his hearing aids until he was about two years old. Nevertheless, the combination of parental devotion and Anthony's innate abilities have resulted in high-level language and intellectual development. His voice quality and speech, however, reveal that his impairment is very profound.

When Anthony was graduated from his university, he received many high honors. He started his education in a special school for hearing-impaired children, but successfully entered the mainstream during elementary school. He has excelled academically throughout his education. He is employed by a large corporation in a position of importance and responsibility, where he works closely with normal hearing employees. He has recently married a hearing-impaired woman, bought a house, and has his life very well under control. He manages the normal hearing world quite well. His social and leisure-time activities are spent with hearing-impaired friends and a few close normal hearing friends.

Janice is very bright. She is quite articulate with little difficulty in making herself understood, though her voice quality reveals that she has a hearing impairment. Although Janice is profoundly hearing impaired, she was mainstreamed from the beginning of her education. In her secondary school she was the only hearing-impaired student. She came to me for therapy because she was painfully self-conscious and socially isolated. When a group of hearing-impaired teenagers organized, Janice became a faithful member. She was very grateful for her new social relationships. Janice went to a college for hearing students. There she became very involved with a religious group, different from her family's religious background. Her new affiliation gratified her needs for acceptance, despite the family conflict it generated. She now attends graduate school.

Paul is twenty-four-years-old and mainstreamed from nursery school. His language is quite good, but his speech and voice quality underscore how profoundly hearing-impaired he is. He excelled in school and won several awards for academic excellence and many scholarships for his higher education. Paul transferred from a college for hearing-impaired students to one for normal hearing students, because he wanted to have more opportunities to use his voice and his language, have more meaningful communications, and be in a more normal environment. He maintains friendships both with hearing and hearing-impaired friends.

Grace has a profound hearing impairment. Her voice quality is poor. However, her language is excellent and her speech is good. She is very bright and attractive. She is well educated, has two graduate school degrees, and a challenging job. When told by the counselor at the residential school for the deaf she attended that she could not succeed in a college for hearing students, she took the challenge. With much personal pride she ridicules the short-sighted counselor.

Grace is very proud and very aggressive in pursuit of her goals. Sometimes a little too aggressive, she overwhelms some of the hearing-impaired people she knows. She seems to get along better with her normal hearing friends who include her and with whom she actively socializes. She keeps herself active, pursuing new challenges to ease the frustration in her quest for an enduring and meaningful heterosexual relationship.

Robert at sixteen is angry about everything. His anger is more than ordinary adolescent anger. He cannot make himself understood and does not accept school efforts to help him with his communications skills. He has a severe-to-profound hearing loss. He is unattractive. He refuses to wear his hearing aids. He rejects his school and his fellow hearing-impaired students. He rejects the members of his family who view him as unsocialized and spoiled.

Robert's father died when he was five. His father was very patient with him and was his foremost advocate. Robert has not recovered from losing him. His grief is profound and his rage is overwhelming him and everyone else who has to deal with him.

Jessica has no available articulate verbal language. Any verbalizations are incomprehensible. She is embarrassed to use her voice. She can communicate only through sign language. She cannot write very well and is probably illiterate. She attended a residential school for the deaf from the age of three until she was twenty in a state far from her family's home.

Jessica's family had little to do with her education. They have not accepted her and seem to be ashamed of her. No one in her family has learned to sign sufficiently well in order to communicate with her. Jessica perceives the rejection. She is also without friends and any gratifying social relationships. She is severely depressed and isolated.

There are hearing-impaired people whom I do not know who communicate through manual language, lead satisfying lives, and have self-fulfilling careers. I have not discussed them. In these brief sketches I have tried to introduce you to some hearing-impaired young people I have known personally. Each of them represents what can happen in the process of growing up hearing impaired. Like all human beings, hearing or not, they have had their share of struggles. Some of them are doing as well as many other people their age, irrespective of the presence of their disability. Some of them are just about surviving. After this overview, it becomes important for us to see how we can smooth the road enough for your child, so that whatever rough spots he encounters he can navigate them with success.

The Mainstream Approach Or the Special School for the Deaf: Which is Best Suited to Your Hearing-Impaired Child?

The school where our children start spending a significant portion of their daily lives is entrusted with educating them with more than just academic information. At school our children have the oppportunity to exercise their social and emotional skills along with their brains to develop themselves. Therefore, the choice of school for our hearing-impaired children is crucial.

Not only do we want them to get a good education, we want them to be exposed to the type of education that they can assimilate. It is fine to have classes for the gifted, enrichment programs, and language labs with tapes for learning foreign languages. However, if our child is not gifted or cannot benefit from the use of electronic equipment, the program is not relevant.

One of the issues for parents of the hearing impaired is whether a special school for the deaf is better suited to their child than mainstreaming in the neighborhood school. Much depends on the child and the resources the child brings to the educational environment. Questions related to the level of the child's language development should be raised first to gather information before a decision can be made. Is there sufficient language development to receive instruction in a regular setting? Is some form of special education needed?

It is also important to consider if the child has the emotional resources to cope with an intellectually challenging environment geared to normal hearing students. A bright or average hearing-impaired student might fare better emotionally and academically in an environment that establishes individual goals for him. Of equal importance is whether his level of social skills would allow gratification in his social interaction with classmates. We want to choose an environment that will enrich his experience and foster his growth, not one that will overwhelm him or bore him.

The Advantages of Being in the Mainstream

In 1975, Public Law 94-142 was passed to improve the educational prospects for disabled and handicapped children. It called for providing all such students with the "least restrictive environment" [1] essential to insure a satisfactory education. As a result, school districts were encouraged to keep their hearing- impaired students within their home districts, if the students were capable of benefitting from a "normal" educational experience.

As a support to those students who remained in their home districts, resource rooms with special education teachers were established to provide remedial help. Other students like Stephanie received assistance from an itinerant teacher who spent one period a day at her school to provide tutorial help. This teacher also recognized the importance of coordinating her efforts with Stephanie's classroom teachers. Therefore she spent additional time conferring with them. For some students who are manual communicators, sign language in-

---

[1]/It is important to note that the definition of "least restrictive environment" is undergoing change and that the mainstream is not always viewed by all educators as least restrictive. Irrespective of whatever new perspectives develop, it is most crucial that the educational environment be the most appropriate one tailored to the needs of the hearing-impaired child·

terpreters have been provided to translate simultaneously the teacher's instruction into signs.

By keeping students in the mainstream, an opportunity was provided to help them integrate into the world of their normal hearing peers. The hearing-impaired students capable of being in the mainstream experienced a broader range of people, including other students with other disabilities. Students without ostensible problems could also experience and learn to accept disadvantaged students. The plan was democratic and broadminded.

Factors That Make Mainstreaming Work

From my experience with the "least restrictive environment" objective, it is the administrators, teachers, and parents who determine its benefits to the student. The involvement and committment of the school staff to actualize the mainstreaming concept for the student is what makes this work well. Teachers and administrative personnel need to make some adjustments to assist the hearing-impaired students. These are not excessive. If presented carefully, most school personnel appreciate that some of these adjustments can be generally helpful to all their students.

The Little Things Make the Difference

The major adjustments for staff include recognizing that the hearing-impaired student hears with his eyes and ears. Therefore, the teacher needs to face the hearing-impaired student when speaking to him individually or to the class. To speechread the teacher the hearing-impaired student should be seated in class toward the front and off center for the best perspective and out of the glare from sunlight. It is important that the teacher refrains from speaking while writing on the chalkboard with her back to the class. Especially helpful during group discussions is the teacher who will point to and call the name of a speaker she is recognizing to give the hearing-impaired student information to identify the person.

A hearing-impaired student will need a notetaker in those classes where students take their own notes. He will not be able to write and listen at the same time. The teacher can be very helpful by enlisting a student to do this. The helping student and the hearing-impaired student can arrange the procedures to copy the notes: e.g., using pressure sensitive carbonless paper under their own note paper or a copying machine after class. Notetaking requires very little from the notetaker that he would not be doing for himself. It can also be a very gratifying experience to be helpful, for which the notetaker might receive service credit if the school has such a program or some form of recognition. Finally, teachers who use audiovisual materials could provide the manual that describes the materials beforehand so the student can be prepared by a resource teacher for what he cannot hear.

Parents play a very important role in executing the mandate for a "least restrictive environment." According to the law, they must be satisfied with, and affix their signature to, the required Individual Education Plan (IEP) designed for their child. Therefore, they should provide input along with the professionals as the plan is designed. Their child will benefit from their arranging careful placement with the teachers best suited and most willing to work with their child. Parents are well advised to have the committee, working on their child's plan, assign a staff member to coordinate their child's program and services. This person should be available to help staff, parents, and student in the event of problems.

Conferences are held periodically to evaluate how well the plan is being fulfilled. This arrangement has built into it much to help the mainstreamed hearing-impaired child, **providing everyone holds everyone else accountable to it**. Parents therefore should recognize their power and use it judiciously.

From the perspective of the student's social development, the school staff is very important. The extra-curricular staff and the guidance counselors can significantly help the hearing-impaired child integrate by reaching out to him themselves. They can also help by encouraging helpful students to reach out and include the hearing-impaired student in programs of potential interest.

There is a very significant advantage to mainstreaming that happens by virtue of the fact that the hearing-impaired student is present in a normal everyday environment. There are procedures and processes, rules and expectations, and patterns of interaction both formal and informal that the student observes and to which he is expected to conform. These are part of life and as important as academics and extra-curricular programming. To derive full benefits from being present requires an alert youngster willing to participate.

The Importance of Your Child's Reaction to Mainstreaming

How your child feels about being mainstreamed is a very impor-tant consideration. If mainstreaming is clearly the most appropriate placement and your child is enthusiastic or even just willing, you can proceed. However, if your child has some anxiety or resistance, he needs to be helped to accept mainstreaming. This may require your support, support from school staff if he is leaving a special school to enter the mainstream, and a sincere welcome from the mainstream school. A professional counselor or therapist to ease the transition could be very helpful during this time.

I have noticed a significant difference in the capacity of hearing-impaired people to communicate in a group. This process is often difficult for hearing people as well. Often we see people interrupt the speaker, lose interest and drop out of the conversation if not physical-ly then mentally, try to engage another in a private conversation, or make distracting comments, etc. The hearing-impaired person in a group situation may struggle even more because of his inability to lo-cate the speaker easily by just hearing. The normal hearing person can hear the speaker and listen to him without looking at him and recog-nize who is speaking by the tone of the voice. This is not possible for the hearing-impaired person who is in a large group or class.

Those students who have been educated in the mainstream seem to be better able to remain a participant in an orally communicating group. They seems to have more perseverence and greater skill at developing means for localizing sounds and enabling the members of the group to assist them in participating. I have noticed that whenever I have had a visitor for dinner who has been educated in a school for the deaf, that person usually cannot join in the conversation. Instead, almost unaware that there is a group conversation, the person drops out or seeks to pull a member of the group aside. I have noticed that such a person is also unable to allow a third person to join the conver-sation. Certainly, we all know hearing people behave the same way. However, the hearing-impaired person with the experience of being in the mainstream has extensive opportunities to develop the social skills involved in oral (verbal) interpersonal communication with more than two people.

While the hearing-impaired person is being exposed and socialized in the mainstream, it is important to note there are tremendous demands on him. The student must attend with extra effort in order to conform minimally to requirements. I often thought about why Stephanie slept so well at night. After five hours of visual double time and full use of her residual hearing, she certainly craved a good night's sleep.

This effort to "hear" and process communications explains why hearing-impaired students choose athletics and the visual or creative arts as electives or extra-curricular activities in school. Both require more motor involvement and much less verbal behavior. They also provide a physical and creative release of energies where the hearing-impaired child is not disadvantaged.

Advantages of Being in a Special School for the Deaf and Disadvantages of Being in the Mainstream

While the mainstream provides richer and more complex academic and social experiences, it does not provide the student with the continuous special education or the extensive suppportive services he may need throughout the school day. The pace in the mainstream usually is geared to the average students in the class. If the hearing-impaired child is moving slower than the average, he may get lost because of insufficient opportunity for reinforcement, or because he has information-processing problems.

In the special school, students often repeat work or remain at a particular level for a while. It is not uncommon for them to complete high school at nineteen or twenty. Furthermore, the pace of instruction is more likely to be set at the student's rate of learning and need for repetition and reinforcement.

In the mainstream there are not that many hearing-impaired people. In most school districts the hearing-impaired student is not likely to find many students with his specific problem. In a special school for the deaf everyone there shares a common disability. Instead of being one of few hearing-impaired students in the mainstream, the child in the school for the deaf is surrounded by others just like himself. The sense of being different because of a hearing impairment is not a problem in the special school where everyone has a hearing impairment.

Parents want the most comprehensive and appropriate educational environment for their hearing-impaired child. Often they view the mainstream as the educational environment of choice. However, instead of being enriching for some hearing-impaired children, the academic and emotional conditions may be very stressful. For some hearing-impaired children the mainstream may be severely restrictive and unrewarding, while the special school for the deaf may be a nurturing and more appropriate place.

Should You Choose the Mainstream or the Special Education Program for Your Child?

When hearing-impaired children are three years old and ready for nursery school, parents are confronted with their first decision: either the mainstream or the special education program. Your child's audiologist, speech therapist, and your family counselor will provide important input about their perception of your child's educational needs at this time. Friends and relatives may also give you helpful advice as well.

Most of these people will encourage you to choose the mainstream, if it suits your child. The mainstream is useful to your child if he has the capacity to benefit from a regular program. You want your child to **grow within the program**. You do not want him in a place where he may be so lost that its enrichment has no effect on him. Nor do you want him in a program where he will not be stimulated to grow.

It is possible your child may need the special education setting because he does not have enough language or social skills to adapt to a mainstream program. He may require more of nursery school teachers than they are willing to provide, given the individual needs of the other children and the needs of the group. He may require from the teachers skills they are not trained to provide.

You probably know better than anyone if your child has the fundamental abilities to adapt to and utilize a mainstream nursery school program. If you believe your child should be given a chance in the mainstream, then you must make that decision and obtain a place for him. If you are uncertain, then you may want to find a nursery school and consult with the director.

If you are sure your child requires special help, it is wise to choose a special environment. Hopefully, the program you choose will let you know **when** he is prepared to move into the mainstream. In my county there is a special program for hearing-impaired nursery-school-age children. This program requires that the participant attend a mainstream nursery school for part of the week, as well. Such an arrangement might suit your child, if he is not ready yet for the full mainstream program.

I am a proponent of the mainstream educational environment for every special child capable of making a minimal adaptation **and** capable of using the experiences to grow. I define "growth" very liberally as the child's being capable of moving forward one step beyond the point at which he was shortly before. I define "adaptation" as being capable of participating in a setting without being a destructive force.

The early childhood program you select for your child will be one of your child's most important educational experiences. It will provide a foundation for all the other educational experiences that will follow and it will begin to define who he is and where he fits in.

Fostering a Healthy Sense of Self Through the Early Childhood Years

For the hearing-impaired child the benefits of his early childhood educational experiences form the foundation to his further development in his educational and social world. Enrichment is a critical element in his life's experience. It serves to compensate for the inevitable limitations with which he is confronted by his hearing impairment. Normal hearing children should be afforded enrichment in the form of early childhood education. However, your hearing-impaired child **must** have the enrichment of early childhood education to compensate for his impairment.

Early childhood education provides the opportunity to contact the world ouside the family. The nursery school serves as an introduction to the kind of educational structures that are characteristic of "schools" which will be a major part of your child's world at least through his teens. Negotiating the academic scene is a skill that needs to be mastered. The preliminary lessons start with nursery school.

In the nursery school opportunities abound for dealing with peers and authority figures. There are scores of intellectual, creative, and social challenges. Attendant to these opportunities are interpersonal situations with peers and authority figures that address the issues of cooperation, conformity, opposition, acceptance, rejection, etc.

What is special about nursery school is that it provides a supportive environment to learn social skills which otherwise might be learned with great difficulty or not at all. In the protective environment of the nursery school every child must deal with the interpersonal tasks of coping, responding, encountering, reacting, managing, negotiating, mastering, etc. The beginnings of these vital social skills and many fundamental concepts on which academic learning is based are being formed.

This is a time when your hearing-impaired child needs every opportunity to practice and develop as many competencies and master as many skills as possibile to help him meet the next set of developmental challenges in the elementary school. During this time in the mini-world of the nursery and in the mini-world of the play-date or outside on the sidewalk, your child will be utilizing his resources to manage his life without your immediate presence. Confidence and self-esteem grow from positive experiences, while emotional wounds emanate from personal defeats. The nursery teachers try to help the child learn the invaluable social skills in a protective environment. They are probably less inclined to give the stifling overprotectiveness we parents might impose.

Your child's peers also serve as teachers. Nursery school children tend to be rather egocentric. Their play is more parallel than interactive and cooperative. However, through the two years in nursery school there is an increasing social maturity. Children have powerful influences on one another socially. They have an increasing capacity for more cooperative interactions. Sometimes we parents may resist the influences of friends on our children. We need to appreciate the importance of sharing our child with the others, his teachers and his peers, who will help shape him up to fit in his world.

Choosing the Nursery School Best Suited to Your Child

Language lessons, enrichment experiences, and speech therapy should continue during early childhood. However, nursery school should take equal importance. It is an opportunity to become further socialized beyond relationships in the family and the neighborhood block, in an organized environment, where people other than parents are establishing routines and requiring a reasonable degree of cooperation. One might say this is part of the socializing or civilizing of children so that they have the skills to integrate themselves into their everyday environments.

Those of us who appreciate the importance of nursery school could become anxious that the school of choice will not accept our child because of his hearing impairment or immaturity. It is best to leave that anxiety aside and retrieve it only if the school rejects your child. Instead, muster your energy to locate a good school that will enroll him.

Visit Several Schools Before You Choose and Observe Them Carefully

How to pick the right nursery school is a very challenging task. Before you even consider presenting your child to the director of the school, it is wise for you to visit several schools, observe the classes, and compare them. Start by observing the teachers. Pay careful attention to how they interact with the children. Notice what the teacher does to enable the children to have positive, growth producing experiences. Try to determine if there are teachers you think have the skills to provide language enrichment for your child. Language enrichment is a vital part of any school experience. Expecting the teachers to be skilled in this area is reasonable.

Make note of the materials that are available for play. What kinds of free play projects are provided for the children? Consider how the teachers provide discipline and structure for the children, especially the immature, non-conforming, aggressive, and withdrawn children. How do the teachers use the space in the room? How do they teach the children? Do they provide experiences and participate with the children? Do they stand back or lecture?

What Is the School Director's Philosophy?

Take time with the director to explore the school's philosophy of education. Does it encompass the values expressed in the previous section? The director supervises the teachers and seeks to guide them toward the school's philosophy. Next to your child's teachers, she is a very important person.

What Does the School Expect of the Parents?

Learn about parent involvement. It would be in your child's best interest if the school saw you as an important part of the early education team. Teachers and director might be more inclined to let you help them learn how to effectively help your child. Try to learn what the director thinks about mainstreaming. Learn if the school has a mental health consultant and what role that person plays. You may find this person to be a valuable advocate for your child.

If you are satisfied with what you have seen and heard, you may be ready to tell the director about your child. You will want to communicate why you believe her school will be well suited to your child's early childhood education needs. You will also want to help the director consider that the teachers and the other children will benefit from having the opportunity to know your child.

If you like the school and can communicate how terrific you feel your child is, the director probably will be interested in meeting your child to determine if he can benefit from the school's program. During that observation the director will be observing how you interact with your child. This will serve as an example of what your child requires.

If your child has sufficient receptive vocabulary to cooperate with you, the nursery school staff will observe that you are interacting in a manner very similar to a good nursery school teacher: face-to-face, eye-to-eye, with focused attention, and verbally. If your child can cooperate, he will not be a burden but will provide an opportunity for the staff, the other students, and for himself, to grow.

It is very advantageous if the school has more than one class at each age level. This provides the director with the opportunity to choose the teacher that might enjoy working with your child. This should be a teacher who would welcome the experience of working with a special child for her own professional growth as well. It could also be a teacher who has already had experience teaching special children.

If you find that the director of the school you have chosen believes your child will not benefit from the school's program, it is very likely that the teachers will not be able to meet your child's needs. However, it is possible this could simply be unwarranted anxiety on the part of the director and/or teachers. If this is expressed directly in terms of uncertainty that the teachers are equipped with enough experience, you may want to explore with the director a conditional acceptance. This kind of acceptance could be monitored by periodic evaluations to determine if the placement is satisfactory. It is preferable that your child is enrolled in a program directed and staffed by professionals that view themselves as capable of meeting your child's needs.

If your child is not ready for the mainstream there are special nurseries available for the disabled which you should consider. While a special school is likely to accept your child, you should explore more than one program. Critically evaluate its basic philosophy, before choosing the one you think best suited to your child.

Conclusion

During this early childhood period your youngster will be getting wide experience from you and in school about listening, talking, sharing, and being aware. Your child will also be learning to play. In all likelihood the normal hearing children in his life will be raising questions about his hearing aids, his speech, and even about his hearing impairment. This is all likely to happen when you are not present. You will need to trust the teachers to help your child help the other children understand and benefit themselves from his presence in their class. One of the most important advantages to the other children when a disabled child is mainstreamed, is that they can learn about disability. They can also develop the humanitarian values that will be good for them and make the lives of your child and other disabled people slightly easier socially.

The challenge of preparing your hearing-impaired child for the world is awesome. You cannot do it alone, despite your crucial importance. You are wise to construct a network of professionals who will assist you with your goals for your child. As nursery school years near completion the teachers and other professionals involved with your child will be in a position to join in deciding if the mainstream or a special education environment is best for your child.

This is likely to be one of your last major unilateral decisions on behalf of your child's formation of his identity. Hereafter, your child will be in the driver's seat reacting to and stimulating his environment and the people in it. He will be enmeshed his own very individual struggle of figuring out who he is and where he belongs.

Chapter IX

How to Weather the Challenges from Infancy Through Adolescence

I have known many parents, myself included, who have admitted to being overwhelmed with an impulse to resign from parenthood. The urge to abandon ship has been known to begin as early as infancy, particularly with parents whose babies suffer from colic or "infantile insomnia," or during the toddler years with the advent of the "terrible two's." There are some stout-hearted souls who may not be afflicted with "escapism" until later with the sulking of the nine-year-old period or the mood changes of the pre-adolescent. However, by the onset of adolescence when faced with their child's grand rebellion, parents can become consumed with the wish to escape.

The impulse to resign becomes more intense, as the children and their problems get bigger. Increasing numbers of parents would love to actively lobby for legislation to prevent "parent abuse" inflicted by "abusive" children. "Parent abuse" consists of kids dumping on parents the stresses and tensions they are subjected to daily as they try to grow up.

Today I received a note from the mother of an adolescent patient of mine which is a case in point:

Dear Ellyn,

> I have learned all about children dumping, first from you...and now all by myself. I am rebounding from alternate dumping and declarations of independence. I think I'll go shopping tonight. That should do wonders for my battered psyche. [She concluded] ...I am weary and worried. Please help.

It is inevitable that by the time children reach their third year of life parents slowly begin to lose their idealized status of being the most important person in their child's life. By later childhood, though hopefully no later than pre-adolescence, parents need to be prepared to relinquish their seat of honor to the "best friend" and/or the "group."

There is great turmoil in the fantasy of resigning from parent hood, since fine quality substitute mothers and fathers are in small supply. Parents seeking to resign, however desperate they feel, are not apt to pass their "treasures" into the hands of just anyone. So it makes the greatest sense, since there is virtually no easy way out, to learn what developmental challenges our youngsters have ahead of them, because the challenges lie ahead of us too. In this way we will be better able to help them deal with the events that will confront them. It often happens that when we know of the challenges beforehand, it is possible to solve some of the problems that arise or even prevent some of the difficulties.

In this chapter we will investigate the characteristics of each of the developmental periods through adolescence and consider the challenges to hearing-impaired kids (and their families) along the way from babyhood to "personhood." In this pursuit it will serve us well to be humble. We are concerned with the hearing-impaired child for whom there are challenges that we can never know, unless we too are hearing impaired. No matter how we try to empathize with their impairment we will never know it as it actually is.

Through the chapters of this book we have shared the pain and sorrow and the difficulties of being the parents of hearing- impaired children. However, we have not yet confronted the anguish of our children themselves in their private moments of suffering the tragedy of being hearing impaired. I am reminded of a lesson learned from a patient of mine who had suffered actual physical abuse at the hands of her alcoholic mother. She seemed to resent my efforts to understand her pain and rejected any belief I ever had about being able to appreciate her plight. She had suffered and paid greatly for the tragedy in her life. She taught me that however I may have suffered in my life too, I could not be so presumptuous to believe I could feel (empathically) her individual, specific pain for which she had, and was continuing, to pay so greatly.

So I believe it is similar with our children. There is no question that as their parents we have suffered in our own idiosyncratic ways. We can commiserate with other parents, if we care to. However, we cannot know the tragedy of the deprivation of hearing, even if we have a simulated experience. We would be presumptuous and misguided to believe that our tragedy in giving birth to and rearing an impaired child is equivalent to actually undergoing the disability itself. At best we can hope that our compassion and empathy can support our children in their task of negotiating the difficult challenges of our society.

There are other complications. In many ways growing up today is different for our children compared with our own years of growing up. Life in our society keeps getting more complicated and more difficult. For each new generation the technological changes alone alter our society and culture significantly.

I am shocked into this recognition whenever I shop for toys for the six-to-ten-year-old children with whom I do play therapy. Some of the classic games are still on the shelves like Checkers, Parchesi, Husker Du, Monopoly, etc. Then I am confronted by the electronic versions of games like Battleships or electronic games like Simon. These are still manageable for an old timer like me. However, when I encounter the electronic games that require hand-eye coordination with instantaneous reaction times and the capacity to discern which extra-terrestrial symbol is the enemy and which is my partner, I am humbled. This is also the age of the computer which our children will use with the ease we used typewriters, but which many of us uninitiated experience with uneasy incomprehension.

Appreciating that life is significantly different for our children than it was for ourselves may enable us to be somewhat more broad-minded. This may enable us to be more realistic, as we seek to impose our values on their world. They are immersed in a powerful "youth" culture. It has been formulated in some respects with the intention of repelling the adult authorities and influences surrounding them in an effort to establish their separate identities.

Some Basic Conceptual Equipment for Steering Your Child Through a Healthy Infancy and Toddlerhood

By the time your baby has completed the nine months *in utero* he has known the bliss of an almost perfect environment. Your infant was living in a kind of nirvana, where he simply existed while his nurturant needs were fulfilled without an utterance and with no demands from any external source. The rude delivery into the world consisting at the very least of a bumpy trip downward (hopefully without complications), accompanied by a slap on the rump and the discomfort of temperature changes, heralded a taste of what life could be like at times in this new environment.

At this beginning probably before you knew about the hearing disability, your infant just as every other infant, required keen responsiveness to his needs. This responsiveness usually results in a continuation of the "symbiotic" relationship characteristic of the pregnancy for a little while longer, as you attended to your infant's basic needs for food, protection, sleep, and bodily care. The challenge to parents during this time is understanding your baby's primitive needs without the benefit of any rudimentary system of communications. In some ways the parents of an infant, especially a hearing-impaired infant, become a mirror capable of reflecting their infant's needs. With keen attunement to these needs, parents extend themselves to gratify and nurture their infants.

The process of trying to understand emotionally, almost as if you were in the skin of the baby and able to mirror his feelings, is empathy. This willingness to achieve this keen sensitivity is sometimes considered a parental instinct. This attunement tends to last longer in the relationship between the hearing-impaired child and parents.

However, it is crucial that parents recognize that mirroring should not mean automatic gratification for the hearing-impaired baby.

Mirroring for the hearing-impaired child can mean expressing aloud in babbling sounds your baby's need for play and communication with another person. It might also be expressing what your impressions of your child's needs are in the appropriate words, e.g., "Timmy wants to eat," "Jenny feels cold. She wants her blanket," or "Carrie wants to play with her teddy bear. Let's give him a hug." In a way it is simply saying for your baby what you think he means, since he cannot yet express himself directly.

During these early months, if you have succeeded in parenting effectively, your baby may come to **feel** very powerful. You have understood well and your baby benefits from the **sense** of security and profound affection your empathy and keen understanding have provided. However, this delicate super-responsive arrangement exists just so long as it is needed. With the passing months your infant begins to mature. Your baby becomes less helpless and increasingly more competent as his needs become more complex. It is unlikely under these "healthy" circumstances that you could continue to mirror as effectively as you were able. Now your baby is developing an increasingly more complicated inner life.

As you are apt to become less of a perfect mirror during the latter part of the first year, your baby begins to discover that just wishing does not make it so. Your baby may find you are not always capable of gratifying or even willing to gratify his needs by being "Johnny-on-the-Spot" with feedings, diaper changes, a soft blanket or a warm hug. Occasionally, your baby must wait or be frustrated in his wish. He may also be disappointed. These experiences can lead to very strong feelings of dismay expressed in the fury of intense anger and tears commonly known as tantrums. It may seem that all this fury is about the frustration of not having immediate gratification. In all likelihood this is the case, at least in part. And these feelings should also be stated for your hearing-impaired baby. For example, "Danny is angry, Mommy said 'No.'" This begins the process of helping your baby learn an emotional vocabulary, its inflections, and its tones.

However, the frustration and anger that even tiny infants are capable of experiencing, may also express other important emotional experiences. If our baby were able to talk we might find that the intensity of feelings also relates to the **sense of disillusionment** felt about the loss of the sublime feelings of gradiosity. Equally disturbing is the developing awareness that he is not the all-powerful center of the universe whose needs can be gratified by simply wishing.

It is important that we do not grant our baby more adult awareness than he actually has. I am not proposing that your baby has a capacity to articulate these rather sophisticated adult concepts, nor do I believe it is easy for adults to entertain such concepts for themselves. However, it is so important that as parents we come to appreciate that our adult feelings disappointment, disillusionment, grandiosity, narcissism, strivings for mastery, and separateness begin early in infancy and grow in dimension as we mature. Our baby's sense of hurt or narcissistic injury to his infantile sense of power is part of the long process of discovering in a non-verbal way that he is separate from you and his wish cannot (always) be your command.

There is a challenging, fascinating world into which your baby must learn to fit. In order to feel comfortable, it is necessary to develop knowledge and skills to adjust to and fit into his environment. Fortunately, during this first year along with these rude awakenings that power is limited and he is not omnipotent are wonderful physical developments which are also part of the process of maturation. These developments are independent of capacity for hearing. Your baby will learn to raise his head, then neck and upper torso. He will roll over and sit up. This will be followed by creeping, crawling, and standing. Some babies manage to accomplish the mastery of walking before one year of age, and others take as much as eighteen months to move themselves about on their feet. In the realm of physical development your hearing-impaired child is very likely to progress quite normally.

The only area in which there is usually a notable problem directly related to his hearing impairment is in the capacity to locate the source of a sound. The capacity to identify the source or the location of the sound is very difficult, especially if the impairment is severe. To this extent motor tracking and the physical activity like head turning, visual pursuit, and other movements that would accompany auditory tracking behavior will be reduced and be more dependent on visual stimuli instead.

As your baby develops these motor skills, he obtains a new and different perspective on the world, seeing it from more than one point of view. Hopefully your baby will be able to use these developing capacities for perspective as he grows up to entertain abstractions like ideas, values, facts, etc. from different points of view as well.

This capacity to experience the world from varying perspectives fosters the sense of separateness. The expanding capacity for movement and physical self-control enables the fairly healthy, reasonably confident, curious toddler to move away temporarily from his parent to explore the immediate surroundings and eventually a little bit more, expanding his awareness of the outside world. The initial movement toward the outside is temporary and followed by the toddler's need to re-connect with the parent. If your toddler discovers that you are a reliable parent and can be depended on to be available, then he is more than likely going to venture out again to discover more of what the world holds. Courage and assertion can then be nurtured rather than fear and insecurity.

It usually happens during the latter part of the first year that your baby begins to discriminate between parent and stranger. Usually, only his parent will do at these times. When separation threatens, your baby may actually experience a severe panic reaction which should be taken very seriously. Your baby knows the caretaker he wants. This knowledge combined with the capacity to perceive the environment more clearly and discriminate differences enables your baby to begin to define the differences among the humans in his life. This heralds the developing capacity that will eventually enable your baby to define his similarities with and differences from others, that will be used throughout his life in the formulation of his own personal identity.

While your baby is developing the capacity to discriminate between you and strangers, it is possible to avoid the traumatic reactions that can occur. It is wise to help your baby become well acquainted with a substitute for you long before you will leave your baby to a surrogate's care.

Sometime around the two-year-old period something happens to your wonderful, delightful child. Though it could happen somewhat earlier or later, it usually occurs when toilet training becomes an issue. Some children do not accomplish this skill until they are as old as three years or more, but most children manage this learning during the time between their second and third birthdays. What happens essentially during this period is that occasionally delightful children become "terrible" two year olds. It is not that they are so bad, it is just that they wish to behave differently from what we want. Occasionally we see this in testing the limits, when parents say "no" and children challenge the "rule."

By two years, even if your hearing-impaired child's speech is limited, it is unlikely that your child's intelligence is limited. Your child can understand, if not by words then by reading your body language and your lips, the message "No!." Othertimes, the child asks "why" incessantly. Parents eventually notice after repeated explanations that the game is really the goal of making mommy or daddy respond in some way. All the while we parents thought it was a game of reasoning. Sometimes it is, often it is not.

This wonderful "game" can generate quite an opportunity for teaching language in a most casual manner, if you are just a little bit more clever than your child who is testing the limits of his power. However, we cannot afford to be irritated by our child's power strivings. During these "why" moments, we can engage in conversation about anything our child has asked about. This is a wonderful opportunity to imprint language. We parents need to see the value in playing a game even though parent and child may have different agendas. What is important is that the agendas are not at cross purposes.

Unfortunately, parents sometimes become exasperated when they believe they are being manipulated by a two and a half year old. It is undesirable to end a rather valuable "why" question with "Enough 'why's. You do it because I say so!" or "No more questions!" Instead, it is possible to give your child some power while asserting your own by putting him on notice that you will take two more "why" questions and then move on.

Significant challenges tend to arise, when we parents attempt to encourage the use of the toilet instead of the diaper. This is a task requiring of your child rather thoughtful self-control. Sometime around two years the sphincter muscles of children are within voluntary control. However, the actual achievement of this skill takes training. This is not an easy task for child or parent. Autonomy is the issue, masked in the question of **where** the child should eliminate.

I have treated many casualties of this period, including children who are enuretic (urinate without appropriate control during the day into their clothing and at night in their bed); encopretic (soil their clothing by eliminating feces); extremely compulsive and perfectionistic; and/or very angry and "acting out" destructively. Respecting the need for your child to accomplish a sense of personal control is apt to foster behaviors between you that will enable your child to obtain control with success and personal pride. The use of creativity in the problem-solving process that we discussed in Chapter IV will contribute to success in your efforts to toilet train and encourage self-sufficient feelings at the same time.

This is far more productive than engaging in a continual contest or power struggle regarding whose "will" will be broken or who will win the "fight." In any power struggle everyone loses, even the winner. For the loser the struggle frequently results in the loss of self-esteem and bitterness that may lead to direct or indirect rebelliousness. As parents no victory is worth that damage to our child.

In summary, the early infancy and toddler years extend from birth through approximately three years. This is the launching pad for the lifelong task of defining an identity. This process begins with your providing for your child's basic needs and then enabling your child to begin the challenging process of mastery, separation and individuation. Throughout the paragraphs I have underlined words like "sense" and "feelings" in order to stress that the developing emotionality of your baby is a non-verbal experience. I have already mentioned that it is important that we do not grant our babies more awareness than they actually have.

I am not proposing that babies have the capacity to experience life as we adults do. However, it is so important that as parents we appreciate that emotions begin their development early in infancy and grow in dimension as we proceed through the developmental periods. If we are fortunate, our intellectual or cognitive experiences are accompanied by a breadth of emotional experiences which enrich our lives and make us more humane. The more we are able to expand the experiences of our hearing-impaired children, the more we enable them to compensate for their auditory deprivation.

Substitute Parents: Some Considerations

In view of the importance of enriching and expanding experiences for our hearing-impaired children the question of who will undertake the primary responsibility of rearing our children is a very real one for many parents today. The more traditional family of father, the head of household, and mother, the homemaker, has changed radically. Today it is not uncommon for both parents to work and for a surrogate parent to assume the major child rearing responsiblities shortly after birth or during the infancy-toddler period. There are many normal hearing children and parents for whom this arrangement works, but it is not the arrangement of choice for everyone.

It has been my experience that those children who do not do well with this arrangement are usually not identified until they come to nursery school and manifest adjustment problems, which I am called upon to observe. I usually learn that mother returned to work within the first six months of infancy and that the father took no paternity leave.

Recently I was asked to consult with a family whose five-year-old daughter was expressing rather depressive feelings, soiling her underpants in the daycare center she attended, and physically abusing the children in her group. Her mother who had been the primary caretaker, had returned to work when she was eighteen-months-old. Both parents are teachers. Not all children are as verbal and bright as this girl, who clearly expressed her anger and sadness verbally. She was able to communicate that she missed her mother and father while she was left in the daycare center.

Both parents were disturbed about their child's problems. They were honest about their irritation over how her problems were upsetting their well-worked-out careers. Fortunately they were willing and able to alter their schedules and provide more parental presence and less surrogate parenting.

This, however, is a normal hearing child. For the hearing-impaired child the decision about who will do the caretaking is not so simple. Because the care required is so extensive and vital, especially if the normal and natural development of language is the goal, it is most desirable for at least one of the parents to be the primary caretaker. If a substitute is needed, it is preferable this person be only responsible part-time.

It is possible that an extended family member who is deeply devoted to the child may make a satisfactory substitute parent. It is important that this relative is willing to be educated regarding the child's special needs and special care. A surrogate with maternal warmth and educated in language and psychological development may also serve as a substitute for the parent caretaker. Locating such a person is a rather difficult business.

The problem of who shall be the **primary** caretaker becomes an especially difficult problem, if both parents have careers that cannot be interrupted or if their incomes are vital for the livelihood of the family. However, creative arrangements are not impossible to forge. I am reminded of neighbors who are determined to rear their own baby. They have arranged their schedules so that mother works mornings into the mid-afternoon and father works mid-afternoons through the evening. Their baby is not hearing impaired but has the benefit of each parent taking a equal role in her rearing.

Parenting a hearing-impaired child successfully is a full time occupation which is very demanding, but very gratifying. It is to be hoped for the sake of the hearing-impaired child that both parents are willing and able to take the responsibility and provide the mutual support each has to put forth in their daily efforts. Both are in need of a supportive network of family, friends, and professionals.

There is an important complicating factor that deserves some consideration. It is the concept of the compatibility between the temperaments of the caretaker and the child. A rather energetic parent will probably feel quite at home with with an energetic child. A more complacent parent may view an energetic child as suffering from "hyperactivity." It is not uncommon for some hearing-impaired children to be very active, (i.e., motorically expressive) because they are so frustrated in not being able to effectively express themselves verbally. On the other hand a physically immature child who may not walk until eighteen months may be a great concern to parents who pride themselves on their athletic skills and capacity for physical activity.

It is possible that the hearing-impaired child is better off being cared for by a surrogate parent, when the temperamental compatibility between child and biological parents is very poor. An even more difficult problem arises when parents are so intolerant of their own insufficiencies that their child's hearing impairment becomes an overwhelming and intolerable condition. This could result directly or indirectly in continual rejection of their child. If such feelings of rejection exist, it is most desirable for the parent experiencing them to obtain some professional help to work them out.

However, in summing up this important issue, in most cases it is still apparent that there is probably no one better than parents to give to their hearing-impaired child the needed nurturing. Deciding who will do the caring may never even be an issue for many families and yet for others, it may be a monumental problem.

Early Childhood: Is There More To It Than Just Play?

Absolutely yes! In Chapter VIII we spent a good deal of time investigating the importance of early childhood education. Not all three-and-four-year-old children are enrolled in nursery school programs. However, increasing numbers of children are, and many public school administrators are establishing pre-kindergarten programs because they recognize their importance. For the hearing-impaired child of two-and-a-half or three years there is a great need for the socialization and academic experiences. Early childhood education in a nursery school is a necessity rather than simply a desirable experience for the hearing-impaired child.

Early childhood which begins for our consideration here at about three years, is a time when your child, who has achieved impressive body control, is using this control to master even more challenging tasks like riding a bike, climbing the jungle gym, skipping, running, etc. It is the time when your child should have already learned that you will be easily available, if he is brave enough to wander and explore. Now he can let you out of his sight and go much further away from home to learn more about the world outside the boundaries of the street on which he lives. He can even learn to perceive the world from another "teacher"--a new kind of "parent-authority figure." This capacity to go forward and reach for new experiences, materials, and people is an active and very healthy condition. It needs to be reinforced and nurtured.

As your child moves toward the outside world, he will be experiencing other children and learning from them as well. His teachers will "run interference" in order to help him use good judgment about what ideas and behaviors to adopt. His teachers will not always control what he chooses to imitate from his peers. This, however, is his beginning in the tasks of discrimination and perception which he would not experience, if his world remained tied exclusively to the family.

Probably, the beginnings of decision-making and problem-solving will have begun in your home. In the nursery school, decision making skills are further challenged and expanded as the boundaries of his world and its people expand and influence your child. For example, in nursery school free play is a time for your child to choose among the toys and materials the ones he will experience. He will also be able to choose among his classmates the ones he will befriend. Hopefully, your child will have a life full of many opportunities and many options to choose from.

Early childhood is not only a time of watching and learning from others, it is also a time of creativity. When creative materials are made available, children are inclined to construct their own productions. Paints, crayons, clay, paste, paper, wood and nails, etc. are manipulated into creations that originate from images that come from their inner lives. This is the time when children should be encouraged to express themselves. If they are fairly emotionally healthy, they will respond to this encouragement. They will also continue to do so throughout their lives, so long as what they express and produce is appreciated and valued by people who are important to them. This is a time when self-esteem should be enhanced and nurtured so that children learn that whatever they produce is valuable. Without this encouragement the reservoir of human potential resting in them is apt to go untapped.

This is particularly crucial in the life of hearing-impaired children. They need to utilize every bit of courage they have to extend themselves in a world, where soon they will have to confront the fact that they are at a serious disadvantage. Under these circumstances, a solid self-confidence will counteract the tendency to be tentative and reticent, or, even worse, uninvolved.

Early childhood is also the time, when children try on the roles of the people around them. They engage in imaginary play and become mother, father, neighbor, community helper, doctor, as well as unsavory characters like "bad guy," thief, bully, "bogey man," ghost, or various "evil" TV characters, etc. In each case they are experimenting with these role models as potential identities for themselves. They will consider these models throughout the years until adulthood, when they will make a committment and choose to one for themselves. The "play" is serious: it is the "work" of the child. If it is treated with respect and encouragement, it increases the chances that the work chosen in later life as a form of livelihood will be a more playful, enjoyable, occupation, and a truer form of self-expression..

It is also during these years that the little mind of the child has its share of anxiety. Sometimes it manifests itself in bad dreams, other times in questions about death, and other times it reveals itself in fears of what cannot be seen. In part, this is because children are so matter of fact that they deal better with what they can see. The unknown therefore takes on ominous features.

Sometimes children's fears come from inside them and are projected to the outside. The internal fear of which they are usually unaware becomes a "real" or imagined fear of some event or some thing outside themselves. These fears may represent the inner feelings which they believe, or have been taught, are bad parts of themselves. Usually children have no conscious awareness of these uneasy internal feelings, but definitely want to reject them by placing them outside of themselves. We can help our children relieve some of their anxiety by encouraging them to distinguish between (their) angry thoughts and feelings which are normal and their destructive behaviors which are inappropriate.

Traces of grandiosity from infancy can be a problem here, because this is a time of magical thinking and the fear that wishes can actually come true. It is one thing to imagine a benign wish might come true. It is quite a disturbing matter to imagine some "bad" thought might come true. Bad thoughts do occur in all of us including little children. We adults may know them as fantasies, bad daydreams, or simply fleeting thoughts. Children may think or play out these "bad thoughts" in fantasy games. Bad thoughts might consist of some destructive wish to hurt someone physically, murderous rage in a fit of frustration, or the simple wish to throw a younger sibling out the window and symbolically out of the family.

Children need a lot of help to recognize the difference between a thought and an action. They also need help to see that some of their actions may be undesirable: for example, when they behave badly by hitting or biting someone or wanting to keep all the toys for themselves though there are plenty for everyone. Most important, however, they need help to see that though their behavior is unacceptable, they are not **in themselves bad**!

The difference between good and bad actions may always seem to be connected to specific episodes. This may seem a very concrete affair. Nevertheless, it is important to help your child develop this general capacity to discriminate. Your child needs to be able to reassure himself or alter his behavior, when you are not around to do it for him. Many children with whom I have worked are convinced they are bad because they have been so thoroughly criticized. As a result, they make no effort to behave appropriately. They feel they are bad, and do not realize they have a choice. Once this bad sense of self is established, it is difficult to nurture the responsibility to use self-discipline to behave desirably.

Through all the developmental periods we will consider, the goal is much the same. We want to convey to our child how much we love him so that these inputs are consolidated internally as self-love. **It is as if we make deposits in our children's internal "love banks" with our genuine caring and respect.** The accumulation of these deposits eventually overflow, so that our children are able to give their valuable resources to the people around them. This "generosity" or sharing of their positive resources should build up their self-acceptance and their self-esteem, which, in turn promotes their ability to have a positive impact on the lives of others. This is the loving task of parents during these early years which builds a sturdy foundation, as our children move on to the bigger challenges of the community beyond the block and to the nursery school.

Because the lives of children during this early childhood period are more physically active than verbal, the hearing-impaired child will probably find this the easiest time of his life to gain acceptance and make a satisfying adjustment than during the periods that follow. However, to be accepted into a mainstream nursery school program requires some minimal ability to conform and follow routines. It is important therefore that home life has some order and structure to it and that it provides respect for the feelings and rights of all the family members regardless of age. This experience at home will facilitate your child's capacity to adapt to the minimal social requirements of nursery school. A satisfactory adjustment to the nursery school program will be likely for the hearing-impaired child with some basic social skills, language and speech skills, and an awareness of the importance of communication.

Middle and Later Childhood: There Is No Question That This Is Serious Business

This period of middle and later childhood usually begins when children enter the public school in kindergarten. It continues to preadolescence. The years we will be considering are between five and nine or ten. It is a time when children are feeling somewhat grown up, as they ready themselves for the "rigors" of elementary school.

Until this time the hearing-impaired child is very much a member of the family and closely tied to his parents. In all likelihood, there has been great attachment to parents, especially to the parent of the opposite sex. By the beginning of middle childhood from five through six or seven years these attachments are being resolved. Little boys who have wanted so much to grow up and marry mommy or have mommy all to themselves are able to recognize the primacy of daddy's role in mother's life, and can now defer to their parents special relationship. They can consider emulating dad instead of competing with him as an adversary. Little girls, on the other hand, somehow resolve the desire for exclusive rights to daddy, give up the charming desire for him as husband, and go about emulating their mothers.

The child, who has put his parents in somewhat more realistic perspective, has also developed an ever increasing appreciation of "time." He begins to appreciate that the world into which he will fit extends past the threshhold of his own home. Children see that the school (though it is not "cool" to admit it past seven years) and the community hold the seeds of great interest for the present and future. The child is also better able to entertain possibilities like being grown up and taking more responsibility for behaving appropriately.

As children go off into the world of school work, they are going to be slowly indoctrinated with expectations of discipline and learning. Some children, especially those who have had early childhood education, have a relatively easier time of adjusting to "rules" and "routines." They have an academic vocabulary developed in nursery school so that words like "work," "materials," "problem," "appropriate," "concentrate," "consider," "patience," "cooperate," etc. are meaningful process words with which they have had actual experience.

Unlike many of the teachers of nursery school, the teachers in elementary school have many requirements to which the child is expected to conform. In the nursery school children who did not conform were helped to master the learning process, even if it took the whole year. Only when children are failing to make minimal progress is the nursery-school teacher concerned about whether the child belongs in a regular nursery-school program.

A Hard Day at School Is Just as Stressful as a Hard Day at the Office

We find in elementary school that not all children have the disposition to accommodate to the expectations and authority of the teacher. Those who act out too much are considered behavior problems. Those who have difficulty focusing or learning are thought to have learning problems. Children who have physical disabilities may have individual standards set for their accomplishments, because they are considered exceptional or special. However, if your child is placed in a regular class, irrespective of the special considerations made, he will be expected to conform with at least minimal social skills. Very little flexibility is granted the child who has difficulty measuring up to the teacher's standards of appropriate behavior.

Therefore, the normal hearing child and the hearing-impaired child who comes home after a relatively successful day of fulfilling teacher's expectations will have been exposed to a significant amount of stress. This is **certainly** true for the hearing-impaired child whether he attends a special program for the hearing-impaired within the public school or a school for the deaf. So remember it is likely that your child will need to let off some steam, depending on how taxing his day has been.

Most important, never forget that the hearing-impaired child has the additional stress of trying to keep track of what is going on by utilizing every sensory avenue available to compensate for insufficient hearing. **This is truly an exhausting task.** Understanding this may make it easier to be tolerant when your child arrives home with "an attitude" or has a tantrum. This understanding may enable you to avoid tangling with him by placing further stress on him for more reasonable behavior. Usually, once a child has had the opportunity to let off some steam, he is better able to be reasonable.

Negative outbursts are not always the rule. Offering your child your ear and a snack over which you can listen and he can ventilate his feelings after school, may circumvent after-school tantrums. Presenting "an attitude" of your own or pressuring your child to immediately sit down to do homework oftentimes creates interpersonal conflicts from which neither you nor your child can benefit.

In addition to accommodating to the demands of teachers and being accepted by them, the child is equally interested in being accepted as a likable member of his peer group. This is also a time of increasing competitive feelings and assertiveness behaviors. Losing face, deferring to perceived unfairness, and being "bossed" are not conditions that are easily tolerated as the price for group acceptance. It also occurs during this period, especially with girls, that there is often quite a bit of overt bickering. It is not infrequent for kids to say they are "in a fight." Children tend to team up and either overtly scapegoat a selective few of the more unusual or sensitive children, or reject others in a rather elitist manner.

This can be a very difficult period. The hearing-impaired kid who is not affiliated with a group that will protect him can experience the pain of feeling different and ostracized. Whether hearing impaired or not, the rejected child suffers painfully with sadness, despair, and sometimes a full-fledged depression.

The Value of Extracurricular Programs to Build Self-Esteem Through Non-Verbal Skills

During this period it is still common for parents to have some influence on the extracurricular lives of their children. If the hearing-impaired child is very much alone, it is possible to enroll him in the local soccer or little league team, the neighborhood dance or karate program, the community arts or drama program, or the gymnastics or ice skating lessons, etc. It is possible for him to make friends at these activities. It is also a means of being constructively occupied in activities that are much less dependent on verbal skills than the academic programs at school. The hearing-impaired child can often excel here and earn the respect that may not be easily forthcoming in school. It is possible to make friends at these activities who might extend their friendship beyond the extracurricular acitivity. It is also a means for mothers to make friends which could foster friendships for the children.

I often hear young children talk of their friends when I am told by parents that they are socially isolated. When I have discussed these friendships with them it becomes clear that these are the friendships made through the friendships among the parents. For these children who do not have anyone from school or in the community with whom they feel close, there is much reassurance gained that somewhere there is a special friend who accepts them.

Pre-Adolescence: The Much Underrated Period
of Stress and Difficulty

Up to pre-adolescence kids tend to react directly to what is going on in their environment. They struggle to fit in, be liked, and sometimes identify with or tolerate people they dislike in order to ward off the horror of becoming the scapegoat. There is nothing worse than becoming the "nerd," "fag," or "misfit." Pre-adolescents develop a great concern with their own value and an ever-increasing need and capacity to understand themselves and how others perceive them.

This is a time when having a chum with whom one can relax and explore ideas, feelings, opinions, and fears is a great comfort. The chum becomes a valuable source of information to the pre-adolescent particularly about how he affects others. There is a give and take. The chum puts up with certain characteristics and may complain about other that he finds intolerable. Usually the relationship endures.

In this relationship each partner receives feedback about how he is affecting the other. The information gives the pre-adolescent an opportunity to perceive himself, his characteristics, and his affect on others. The feedback provides an opportunity to consider modifying traits that, if left unaltered, are apt to become entrenched characteristics. These could interfere with having gratifying interpersonal relationships. In the special relationship with a close friend the pre-adolescent can experiment with speaking freely what he feels. Efforts to change can be considered. The language of the heart has a chance to develop. The humanity in the pre-adolescent has a chance for expression.

I have been working with a group of six pre-adolescent girls. At times each one of them is very hard to like or even tolerate. At the very least, they tend to be very self-involved. We have become increasingly intimate and are all agreed that we are going to stay together to play together and work on problems together. This committment to our relationships has led to an investment on improving our relationships. An openness has developed in which everyone has spoken about the others' pleasing and unpleasing behaviors. This has resulted in concerted efforts to change on the part of each member. It is the kind of sharing and changing that can take place during this age period in the chumship, when pre-teens feel involved and loyal to one another.

The growing intimacy generates strong feelings of attachment. The chum is usually a friend of the same sex. Elements of deep affection and love are likely to develop. This does not mean that there is necessarily overt physical affection expressed, although this is possible. It is more likely that strong affectional ties bind the friendship and permit greater sharing and loyalties. These experiences prepare our children for richer lives as they grow. Having had an early gratifying interpersonal experience makes it more than likely they will choose interpersonal relationships again rather than isolation and loneliness.

How to Hear What Is Going on in the Group: A Vital Question for Teenagers!

Also important at this time is membership in a somewhat larger group: e.g., a club or gang. Feeling wanted by the group is very important which at this time gets translated into feeling worthy and desirable. This has an impact on the sense of self-esteem. If we as parents have done our job, we should have filled the love bank full enough to fuel our child's courage to reach out to others. However, in reality the hearing impairment is often an impediment to an easy acceptance by hearing peers. The result may be that unless some of their earlier childhood friendships hold firm as kids realign themselves during this period, the hearing-impaired child may end up feeling left out (at worst) or be included peripherally, at best.

I am reminded of two hearing-impaired brothers who had a different pre-adolescent experience. The older one was a member of a loosely formed neighborhood group of boys who played ball and did other things together. I remember listening to his parents' anguish over his pain, when he was left out or simply overlooked and not included. He was at a disadvantage in that he could not casually **hear** plans being made. Someone had to make a special effort to inform him.

The younger brother, on the other hand, had a very special hearing chum. This chum was very faithful and took very good care of him. They traveled together between the groups of hearing-impiared friends and the hearing friends. This chum served as another pair of ears for the younger brother who has been blessed by this relationship.

When the group gets together, it is extremely difficult for the hearing-impaired member to keep track of the conversation. Being left out is bad. Being in the group and being ignored is not too much better. By pre-adolescence you will have had much experience watching television with your child or having had innumerable family conversations. You may appreciate how much effort you must make to encourage your child to stay with the group. Never forget your effort is still very small compared to the constant effort your child must make, if he is going to enter and remain with the group situation.

Peer Relationships
and the Hearing-Impaired Adolescent

We have considered some of the very stressful realities of peer and peer group relationships. It is not routine for the normal hearing pre-adolescent to be friends with a hearing-impaired peer. Any friendship takes efforts to sustain it. However, the friendship between a hearing and a hearing-impaired person requires even more willingness to **give** help on the part of the hearing person and the willingness to **take** help by the hearing-impaired person. On both sides it is easy to drop out of the relationship because too much energy may be required to sustain it.

At the same time it is important to recognize that this is a time of extreme egocentricity. The kind of giving and empathy required is no small task for the normal hearing and hearing-impaired members of the group. It is probably crucial therefore that the hearing-impaired pre-teen have received as much "love" as is possible, so that when his love bank overflows he has resources to give to his friend(s). In this way he can balance the giving between them.

Having an impairment is particularly difficult at this time because of the great sensitivity to bodily changes that frequently begin during the pre-adolescent period. Secondary sexual characteristics start to form which may create self-consciousness about one's body. This is a time when the mainstreamed hearing-impaired pre-adolescent wants to hide his impairment. Nowadays, hearing aids worn behind the ears are sufficiently powerful for severely and profoundly impaired pre- teens so that the conspicuous body aid has become almost obsolete in this age group.

Many pre-teens consider removing their aids altogether, so there are no "clues" of impairment. Of course, voice quality and articulation suffer greatly when this is done. Some pre-teens are unable to recognize how much more attention is brought to their impairment when they remove their aids. This was a very important struggle for Stephanie which she discusses at length in Chapter X.

This is also the time when your child may confront painfully how he feels about being hearing impaired. You may not hear directly what is troubling him. If you are attentive you are apt to "hear" it through his unhappy facial expressions, the tone of his voice, flatness of emotions, lack of motivation, lethargy, boredom, hostility, etc. All of these conditions may indicate the presence of depression. One of the most difficult parts of being the parent of a hearing-impaired child is witnessing the social tragedy of the impairment, which can involve some very painful loneliness.

From Stephanie's pre-adolescence through adolescence I questioned the decision to help Stephanie to "hear" and speak. I wondered with other parents of mainstreamed children, if it had been in our children's best interest to bring them into a world, where it was inevitable they would be one of the very few articulate hearing impaired among the normal hearing. From my professional work I managed to obtain some answers to this question.

I saw in many of my patients who had normal hearing that loneliness is one of the most painful of human experiences. They would compromise themselves in any number of ways to avoid it. Often these people would experience excessive anguish from their interpersonal relationships, but they would tolerate it because leaving the relationships would lead to loneliness which they found unbearable.

From my patients who attended the schools for the deaf, I learned that within the community of the deaf there are peripheral deaf people, excluded by their deaf peers or by themselves for any number of personal and emotional reasons. Being in the deaf community or attending a school for the deaf is not a guarantee of friendship and belonging.

From Stephanie's friends who were mainstreamed, I learned that those who wish to be in the deaf community to avoid dealing with the discomfort and loneliness they encountered in the mainstream, simply learned sign language very quickly and made friends with those who communicated manually. From pre-adolescence or earlier they could elect membership in community groups that gathered these hearing impaired children together.

From Stephanie I learned that a person with oral skills can learn sign language and can choose to move between the worlds of the normal hearing and the hearing impaired. However, learning sign language did not solve the problem of loneliness for Stephanie, because she seemed more comfortable with oral language and the mainstream. Instead she focused on learning the social skills to develop relationships. This was how she eliminated the loneliness in her life. She will discuss this issue in Chapter X.

Nowadays, I do not question the committment to help Stephanie develop oral speech and language. She has had choices throughout her life which her capacity with language and speech has made possible. She has taught herself to become a socially successful person in much the same way that she taught herself to speechread. I suspect her unhappiness at finding herself alone provided the strong motivation for her to become a very social person.

You may ask, what is a parent to do while his or her child is facing these unhappy feelings? You are well advised to anticipate the occurrence of this unhappiness. It is a fact of anyone's life, though our guilt makes our hearing-impaired child's unhappiness seem more profound for us. You may seek to understand and do your best to empathize, so that when you experience your child's unhappiness or bitterness, it will not come to you as a shock. Then you will be more emotionally available to help.

This is somewhat akin to the experience of commiserating with someone who is mourning. It is one of the most difficult situations to be in because words seem useless. Yet words are all we think we have. A long time ago a young woman whose young husband died of a heart attack helped me to understand. She was disdainful of the "sympathies" from others about her loss. It was not that she disliked the people. She resented their "efforts" to make her feel better. She taught me that there are some conditions about which we can only feel bad. When people try to make it better, they simply make it worse.

By comparison, the tragedy of suffering a hearing impairment is an immutable fact of life. Perhaps we can simply mourn the loss of the normal hearing with our child silently, with tears, through words, or in any other way we feel it. Though we are not the afflicted one, we have also lost and are mournful as well. Bearing witness by listening, nodding, feeling, or just sharing space with our presence may be enough or all we can do. Being silent is sometimes a kind of giving, because the discomfort we ourselves experience results in **two** people **sharing** discomfort.

Sometimes, it is possible after the grieving to ask rhetorically if there is something that could be done to make things better. You will know if your pre-adolescent is open for such a problem-solving discussion, if he reponds with curiosity or interest. If negativism is the response, then being unhappy is what is on the agenda. Being unhappy together can soften the pain.

Adolescence: The Grand Period During Which Identity Is Actively Pursued

The onset of adolescence occurs about the time your child begins to react psychologically to pubescent physical changes and to establish a personal identity. It is not uncommon for this period to begin before the teens are reached or to continue after the teen years have passed.

One reason for extended adolescence is that it is a time of the consolidation of the many developmental "growth" tasks that have arisen since birth. It takes a great deal of fortitude to manage this period which is often dependent upon the success with which a young person has passed through the previous developmental stages. Even for the best-adjusted young people, adolescence is a period of emotional upheaval. For the hearing-impaired teenager, it is as tumultuous and ridden with turmoil as for any normal hearing teen.

Often the adolescence of hearing-impaired teens is extended also, because they require more time to complete their developmental experiences. A hearing-impaired person often requires more time to obtain the full experience of life and process its impact. For every experience, the personal and social elements must be absorbed, understood, and then integrated in whatever idiosyncratic manner the adolescent has developed to see, hear, perceive and think. Everyone, hearing or hearing impaired, processes life's events according to his available resources that include both his strengths and limitations.

The hearing-impaired person is different because of his hearing limitations. But he is very much like the rest of his peers in all the other human dimensions. For all relatively healthy adolescents the developmental tasks do get accomplished. However, it is not uncommon for parents to feel disturbed that their adolescent seems less mature than his hearing contemporaries and does not seem to catch up. They cannot find reassurance in knowing that many normal hearing adolescents lag behind, as well, for a variety of conditions that do not even trouble our children. There should be no concern if our hearing-impaired children seem less mature. They are destined to pass through the same hurdles as everyone else. They will fulfill their potential if opportunities are available to them. In the end what matters is that they do indeed complete their adolescence and not how quickly they do it.

The Struggle to Establish Independence

Adolescence is a time of clarifying a sense of identity and solidifying a basic sense of self, whether one is hearing or hearing impaired. This is partly achieved by establishing autonomy and separateness, tasks toward which we have helped our children strive since birth. This independence is very difficult to achieve, because most teenagers are dependent upon their parents for material resources to fulfill their needs at least through high school. Some of these needs include food, shelter, clothing, recreation, supplies, comforts, and luxuries. Adolescents also depend on parents to fulfill their emotional needs for support, affection, faith, and trust. This is sometimes harder for parents to believe, when their adolescents are ignoring them or dumping on them.

For many who continue into college and for those who pursue a professional or graduate education, there is a good deal of extended dependency. This results in a later consolidation of autonomy by these young people who will someday be quite self-sufficient. In a sense they stay on the parent payroll longer.

During the struggle for autonomy it is very difficult for a adolescent to take from parents without feeling controlled, regardless of the presence or absence of parental expectations. It is also very difficult for parents to give without attaching some strings. Some of us parents equate parenting with guiding and controlling and have great difficulty defining our role in more equal terms.

During this period our children would benefit if we trusted them to have good enough judgment to use wisely the material resources we give. We could benefit too, because this trust would be like implementing the self-fulfilling prophesy that we discussed in Chapter III. It is to be hoped that we have instilled enough problem-solving and decision making skills by this time that thinking about goals and consequences is becoming a habit for them. If it has not, we need to do more problem-solving work which we discussed in Chapter IV.

The problems of dependency are further complicated by the adolescent's conflict of not wanting complete independence. Independence brings freedom, but also responsibilities. Responsibilities create tension and pressure. Furthermore, it is not uncommon for feelings of inadequacy and anxiety about failure to lead to an overwhelming fear of being devastated by independence. A serious conflict often arises in which there is a pull toward separation and independence and an opposite pull to regression and dependence. Some of the typical moodiness observed in teens can be attributed to this conflict.

I remember a sixteen-year-old adolescent who had serious back problems and tension headaches that began in her neck. Her mother brought her to me with the hope that therapy would alleviate the stress causing her physical symptoms. In our work Jane was able to uncover that she felt her mother was always "on her back" worrying about her and guiding her. While she was very angry she suppressed her feelings. This led to continued backaches and tension headaches. As a result Jane's life was very restricted. She rarely engaged in any physical activities and traveled practically everywhere with her mother.

When we discussed what she might do to help her mother "get off her back," Jane made it clear that she did not want to do anything. She admitted that she was not yet willing to give up her mother's protection. She discovered that the insecure part of her still needed to have her mother as her guide, even if it meant continued backaches. She recognized that she had complicated mixed feelings about dependence and independence.

Jane and I ended our regular weekly appointments after two years. She was feeling fine physically, doing well in college, and developing meaningful relationships. We have continued to meet every six weeks for the past year. In our last session Jane told me of her excitement about the ski trip she was taking the coming weekend. This was very daring for a former back patient.

We looked at her relationship with her mother who is currently rather calm about Jane's welfare. We noted that Jane had not reported backaches for over a year. And at the end of our session she handed me her own check. She very proudly told me that she is taking financial responsibility for our sessions, since she is employed and earning money. I have witnessed Jane's adolescent struggle and increasing successes as she gracefully and persistently continues to resolve her independence-dependence conflicts.

The hearing-impaired adolescent who has been very closely guided by his parents throughout his life may feel somewhat like Jane. In all likelihood he feels the reality of the weight of his disability. Like Jane he probably experiences his parents' anxiety about his welfare, which is grounded in their recognition of his impairment. He is apt to share with Jane similar feelings of conflict about independence and dependence, as a result. Overcoming his own anxiety, giving up his parents' special protection, and resolving this conflict about independence and dependence is a very significant adolescent achievement for the hearing-impaired person.

I am reminded of a presentation Stephanie made to high school graduates and parents of hearing-impaired children of assorted ages at the New York League for the Hard-of-Hearing just after graduation from college. She spoke at great length about her apartment in Massachusetts, where she would be living alone while going to graduate school at Tufts University. She was expressing her pride in herself that she was ready to be independent and live entirely alone, unsupervised, and unprotected.

As parents who have worked toward the goal of fostering self-sufficiency, we want to continue this through adolescence. We do not want to sabotage ourselves and our child by rescuing them from this conflict. Independently resolving the conflict is a behavioral expression of voting for one's own independence. We can help by encouraging strivings for independence. If our adolescent stumbles and turns to us, we should be prepared to lend a very sturdy helping hand **momentarily**. But we should remember to support any effort toward his re-mobilizing for independence.

In regard to the parental problem of sabotaging our own goals, my daughter Danika has helped me to understand what a negative effect the "broken record" routine can have. This is a parental affliction consisting of repeating ad nauseum the lessons and values they have taught their adolescents since shortly after birth. In our home it would go like this. Danika would remark casually about a dilemma that might involve a friend or a decision facing her. I would offer parental guidance automatically, doing what I believed was my role. She would reject me and my fairly sound advice and become hostile.

Finally, before it was too late to do us any good, she decided to explain what was happening from her perspective. She explained that by giving her my opinion when it was not directly solicited, I was depriving her of arriving at an independent solution. If my idea was similar to her idea, she felt that instead of doing her "thing" she would be doing my "thing." And she made it very clear that she definitely did not want to do my "thing." In a sense by intruding my opionion, I might force her to choose the opposite of what she really wanted.

It became clear that I was sabotaging our mutual goal: that she become increasingly self-sufficient. I did not know that she only wanted me to listen and be a sounding board, when she considered her dilemma. She did not realize that she needed to be clear about what she wanted from me. Did she want me to listen or counsel? Furthermore, she added, my giving guidance felt like I distrusted her. When I chose to offer my unsolicited opinion, it seemed to her as if I believed she did not have the capacity to solve her own problems.

A hearing-impaired patient, Mindy, was pleased with her self-sufficiency. However, at thirty-four she was very anxious about significant decisions like selling her house and taking an apartment. She turned with each event to her parents for guidance. This seemed sensible at the time.

However from very deep inside, Mindy expressed disconcerting anxiety about her parents dying. Her parents were in fine health, but she expressed a potential sense of personal devastation should they be lost. She worried unnecessarily. Her worry demonstrated to us that she was not as self-sufficient as she thought. In some ways she and her parents seemed to maintain a barely visible thread of dependency. This dependency was maintained by her parents encouraging Mindy to let them participate in her important decisions.

We can undermine independence strivings in our children by subtle or direct inputs that interfere with their independent decision-making. In our own experience we usually know when we have been given information which helps us make an independent decision. We also know when we have been told what to decide. We should monitor when we make decisions for our children. Our goal should be to foster their independent decision-making. Mindy has chosen to deal with this discovery about her dependence on her parents involvement in her major decisions. She wants to give up her painful anxiety and be genuinely independent.

Setting Occupational Goals: The Choice of a Career

Another developmental hurdle is the task of setting occupational goals. This is a time of projecting into the future and working toward preparing oneself for earning a living. The task of achieving in high school in order to enter college is a serious business. Today this task places a lot a pressure on the mainstreamed hearing-impaired student who is expected to produce like everyone else in spite of his limited hearing.

The Scholastic Aptitude Test demands a great deal of effort from an adolescent with an interest in higher education. For hearing-impaired adolescents standardized achievement tests, which are usually high in verbal content, are difficult. This is not an arena in which they can easily compete. Taking these tests serves as a statement of willingness to try to qualify, but brings with it risks of rejection and disappointment.

Fortunately, most mainstream colleges are flexible about the significance of the SAT scores for the hearing-impaired applicant. Some schools waive these required scores altogether. Gallaudet University in Washington, D.C. and the National Institute for the Deaf in Rochester, New York are just two schools in the U.S. established to provide higher education for the hearing impaired. They have well-structured programs with flexible admissions policies for aspiring students.

Some oral hearing-impaired teens will be happy to leave academia after graduation from high school and not go on to college. Often, they elect technical programs in high school. Otherwise, they plan to undertake specialized training after graduation from high school.

There are career goals that are not realistic for the hearing-impaired adolescent, simply because of limited hearing. Many occupations require the use of telephone communications. Until TDD's are more commonly available or other advanced systems of communication are developed, some career choices will be unavailable for the hearing-impaired adolescent, as he considers his future and his career.

On the other hand, it seems from my experience that a capable hearing-impaired person with articulate speech and normal language skills has many career options which are probably limited only by his own interests and motivation. Perhaps it would be unrealistic to consider becoming a patrol officer for a police department, telephone operator or telephone survey interviewer. However, a competent hearing-impaired adolescent could consider being an attorney, a medical doctor, a psychologist, a waitress, a postman, a dentist, etc. Career choices are innumerable for the hearing-impaired person who has the self-confidence, intellectual skills, motivation, emotional and social capacities, and can pass the qualifying examinations.

Jim is a normal hearing 14-year-old patient of mine who suffers from brain damage, resulting in severe verbal-processing problems and poor impulse control. He is able to perceive that his low-average intelligence gives him limitations and prevents him from having the many advantages of his peers and siblings, who are not disabled. His intense jealousy of their opportunities embitters and torments him. This results in violent behavior, because he is consumed by frustration, his own sense of impotence, and poor impulse control.

Jim struggles to learn how to mobilize his aggression and put it to work for himself. He is trying to translate his jealousy into envy so he can imitate the success of others or aggressively find a satisfying niche for himself. His emotional problems deprive him of recognizing his strengths and his small but respectable achievements.

This is a plight from which we need to protect our children. Teaching them how to measure their successes and to be pleased with every step upward can change their focus. Instead of feeling hopeless that they are miles from their goal, they should be helped to recognize that they come a step closer with each small achievement. This style of positive thinking needs to be nurtured from birth, if our children are going to make it work for them.

Physiological Changes

Sexual development with the accompanying emotional and physiological changes poses an challenging developmental task for the adolescent. Hormonal changes affect the sense of body self, the point at which one first connects to the environment. For boys the development of secondary sexual characteristics including voice change, the growth of body and facial hair, and the muscular growth or the delay of any of these characteristics are momentous. For girls the maturation of the body with the development of breasts, the onset of menstruation, and the appearance of body hair confront them with their developing femininity.

Furthermore, what is appropriately feminine and masculine have become issues in our society. The feminist movement is still quite alive, and androgyny or sharing sexual qualities of maleness and femaleness by young males and females is appealing to many adolescents. Beyond the cultural considerations of sex-role definitions that are continually expanding are the issues of sexual expression and freedom. Some adolescents including the hearing impaired use sexual relations to act out their needs for interpersonal intimacy. For some adolescents this acting out feels good. For others, it is the choice because they have a limited appreciation of alternative means to achieve interpersonal gratification.

Friendships and Trust

During this period we tend to see strong committments to friends. Parents often resent this devotion and may even experience jealousy toward the friend. Instead of fault-finding and resentment we parents might consider feeling pride that our adolescent has moved to the level of being concerned with someone else's welfare, no matter who it is. Eventually, this altruism will come home to roost if we do not alienate our adolescents with parental reproaches.

Kate at sixteen years spent her sophomore year in high school very unhappy with her social relationships. She explained to me, though not to her parents, that she was friends with kids who were actively into sex and experimenting with drugs. She pleaded with her parents to send her to private school. They could afford to do this, but they insisted that she remain in the local high school. They believed that whatever her problems were, she would have them anywhere because they were coming from inside her.

Through her therapy Kate worked out the problems with peer pressure. She found she could accept and be accepted by her local high school friends without compromising her own values at all or too much. After this was accomplished, something unusual began to happen. Her mother started to make it difficult for her to socialize with her friends. Kate began to resent her mother's criticism of her friends and her mother's interference with her activities.

Kate confronted her mother at a family session. With frustration and confusion she said, "First you want me to make friends and adjust to high school. I did just that and now you are doing everything to interfere with what you wanted me to do!" Kate's mother saw how she was sabotaging her own goals because she was uncertain about Kate and Kate's friends. We had to focus a good deal on the mother's distrust of these kids, as well as her distrust of Kate's judgment. Mixed in with all this distrust was her fear of Kate's becoming sexually active.

Often adolescents are unpredictable. In times of conflict they might be influenced by our advice or choose the opposite for the sake of being different. Trusting **yourself** to have raised your child well enough may be the foundation for the trust **he** needs to make responsible decisions.

The Adolescent Adequacy Struggle

Among the multitude of concerns confronting adolescents which makes them seem even more egocentric and narcissistic is their preoccupation with their own adequacy. They tend to be very self-conscious as a result. This extends to any human characteristic that is of concern to them. It emanates from their own value system, their reference group, or the value system of someone they admire.

The reference group can be any group of two or more which the adolescent emulates. This is the time of hero worship of celebrities; love for some adult figure other than a parent (e.g., teacher, guidance counselor, friend's parent, older friend, etc.); or aspirations of acceptance by a reference group with which the adolescent wants to be affiliated or has actual membership (e.g., fraternity, sorority, honor society, athletic team, "gang," delinquent group, theatrical group, student government, etc.).

In any case, the actual affiliations or fantasized affiliations often form the model for the values toward which the adolescent aspires. These may be admirable as in cultivating the athletic skills to be on a team or fostering a talent to be the lead in the high school drama. On the other hand, it is possible the goals can be problems such as doing or dealing drugs or acting out, like the kids with motor cycles and chains.

In any case the values aspired to contain the means of measuring personal value, as well. The degree to which the adolescent feels close to accomplishing these values or goals for himself gives him important information about the level of his adequacy. The sense of developing adequacy results in increased self-esteem which expands his self-confidence. These achievements create a sense of self-respect and feelings that others find this "self" likable. It is easier under these circumstances to reach out to others, feeling personally acceptable and thereby, being able to risk that others will be accepting also. From this core of confidence the adolescent is capable of giving of himself to others and receiving in return.

The adolescent's sense of his physical self is only one dimension on which he measures his adequacy every day throughout the day. There are extensive standards about the acceptability of one's appearance. You may ask some of the most attractive adolescents on any day how they are feeling about themselves. You will learn that they feel awful. Conditions that mess up the day vary from "zits" that are forming, to too much humidity, too much weight, not enough muscle, nothing to wear, etc. Preoccupation with the physical self often interferes with interactions with others. By rejecting themselves first they manage to turn inward. They become fearful of reaching out to another, because they expect the same judgment from others that they make about themselves: that is, that they are unacceptable and will be rejected.

Fear of Rejection and the Physcial Self-Image

I remember the day I brought a box of doughnuts to the girls in my adolescent group. We had made a bet the week before, I lost, and the doughnuts were my penalty. Everyone thought it was a good idea until they were confronted with eating in front of each other. Then their extreme self-consciousness about being **seen** "pigging out" was evoked. They admitted the possibility that getting food on their faces also made the thought of eating the doughnuts nearly impossible. It took more than one session for us to learn to eat in front of one another.

Another adolescent whom I saw individually and also in group overdid her sun tanning, and had given herself a bad case of sun poisoning. I must admit that I was moved by her willingness to let me see her and help her work through her physical and emotional pain about how she had almost maimed her lovely face. However, she was not able to come to group and permit the girls she had known intimately for a year to see her.

I have sat with many adolescents who have unburdened themselves about the grief of their daily life. For some it is very difficult to allow the tears to flow, but they do. Though they will use the tissues to dry their eyes, they will not blow their noses. That is the pinacle of embarrassment for many. This is just another example of how self-conscious they are about their bodily functions.

This self-consciousness, which is an adolescent fact of life, extends beyond questions of how one looks physically to how one exists in space. For example, being alone can be a deeply humiliating experience for an adolescent. Being alone with one's parents in public at anytime, but especially on a Friday or Saturday night, is the height of mortification. If the only people to hang out with are mom and dad, then everyone will know what you have been trying to hide behind in your "in" clothes, your cool attitude, your latest haircut, etc. Simply put, they will know you are a loser!

It was never easy for me to be treated in public like a stranger by my children. For a time during their adolescence if we met in town, I could never be sure if I would be greeted like a distant acquaintance or a relative. It did not take me long to stop taking their adolescent struggle personally, and give to them the privacy they needed in public.

Attaining Group Membership

One of the most important adolescent hurdles to achieve is membership in a group --preferably, **not** a group of nerds, faggots, or sleaze bags. Being isolated without a friend is the pits. Having only one friend or being in the group of rejects is not the best solution, but it is better than nothing.

The only adolescents I have known for whom isolation is preferable are those so emotionally disturbed that human contact is traumatic. They are usually in need of serious psychiatric care. So it is very important for us parents to appreciate the importance of friends for our adolescent childen. When we are inclined to be critical of their friends, we need to remember that they represent our adolescent's choices. When we put down the friend, we put down our child. This does not build a sense of adequacy.

I often wonder how painful it must have been to Stephanie when I admired one hearing-impaired friend over another. I was clearly discriminating among those who were well adapted and those who were not doing so well. It is interesting to me now to observe that she was happy to be with peers who were not doing so well, whether they were hearing or hearing impaired.

When I was too close to the issue, I was dismayed because I explained her choices in a very shortsighted manner. I assumed that she had a low opinion of herself, and because of this would choose limited, less "successful" kids. Then I thought she might be so limited herself that only very limited kids would like her. Finally, I discovered that the most likely reason was that she enjoyed being with people she could help and who permitted her to help them.

Initially, I missed seeing that she was taking care of her peers in a manner similar to the way I take care of people. Once I recognized this, I felt respect for her and appreciation of these kids who let her help them. It was not entirely one-sided, they helped her too. On both sides, they were each better for the friendship. Today Stephanie has decided to make a career of helping others which may have been influenced by these early experiences.

Heterosexual Relationships

Once adolescents have achieved some dependable group bonding either in reality, or in some satisfying fantasy with a reference group, they tend to yearn for a one-to-one relationship. They do not always accomplish this development of a boyfriend-girlfriend relationship and the beginnings of emotional and physical intimacy. However, this is a goal. Those who achieve it have begun to experience a level of growth that enriches their interpersonal development. This includes their capacity for mutual dependence (giving and taking) and sharing affectionate and loving feelings. The frustration of these needs make for much adolescent turmoil. It can become another source of bad temper that makes life with an adolescent such a challenge for parents.

For many of my female adolescent patients there is an all-consuming desire to be involved with a boy. Sometimes when our session together is not very stimulating, I watch to see how the interaction goes. Will it die a boring death or will it come alive? At this point I find that there are two topics I can introduce with an adolescent that injects life in them in a hurry: boys and sex. It never fails because these are two main subjects of interest in the relatively "healthy" teenager.

Sometimes hearing-impaired adolescents are somewhat less emotionally and socially mature than their hearing contemporaries. Nevertheless, they eventually experience the full challenges of adolescence. Eventually they too wish for close relationships. Furthermore, they have an additional and difficult decision: shall the much-sought after boyfriend or girlfriend be hearing impaired or hearing. It is a challenge often fraught with disappointment to discover who will respond to them with interest. Although hearing-impaired adolescents tend to gravitate to one another for their intimacies, it is not uncommon for hearing-impaired and hearing adolescents to become intimates. Coupling is a very complex process and probably has more to do with the attraction between two young people than the degree of hearing present.

Hearing-impaired adolescents tend to be as self-conscious as hearing adolescents, often with as much or more reason. For those who are mainstreamed there is a strong desire to deny their major difference and remove the hearing aid, the concrete sign of their hearing problem. Some have difficulty understanding that by removing the hearing aids they only **emphasize** their difference by revealing their speech differences caused by unaided hearing. Speech tends to suffer in quality because of the lack of information from the absent hearing aid that cues clear articulation. The general tone of the voice becomes further impaired. In addition, the capacity to identify environmental sounds that need attention and response is lost to anyone with a severe or profound loss when they remove their hearing aids.

Special Considerations in Friendships
Between Hearing and Hearing-Impaired Adolescents

We have already discussed the special demands on the hearing person in an intimate relationship with a hearing-impaired person. The less skilled the hearing-impaired person is in oral communication, the more is required of the hearing friend. This may be when they are watching television or at the movies. It is very difficult to speechread a person who is not actually present. If the television programs or movies are not captioned or subtitled, the hearing-impaired adolescent often needs help to understand what is happening.

A strain on the relationship can occur because the hearing impaired-adolescent is not able to communicate easily by telephone with hearing friends. So much adolescent living takes place on the phone. This is where ideas are shared at great length, plans are made and changed, and intimacy in a relationship is initiated and sustained.

If there is an extra TDD to loan to a friend, telephone contact is no problem. Instead of speaking and listening, the conversation is typed and produced on the screen of each person. As long as the speakers can type and spell, they can communicate. Not as good but helpful is an arrangement like Deaf Contact. This is a service whereby a third party who has a TDD connects the two friends, only one of whom has a TDD. The contact mediates the conversation by receiving the spoken message from the hearing person and delivering it to the hearing-impaired person through the TDD. Then the contact delivers the message from the hearing-impaired person received by TDD to the hearing person. However, this involves another person in the conversation.

Another technique which produces an even more disturbing intrusion into privacy, is to have a member of the family interpret the call verbatim. In this case the other person is aware that there is a family interpreter helping out. Two phones are set up in proximity. This can be done with a very long extension cord or a wireless phone. The family member communicates the message from the hearing friend on the other end of the line to the hearing-impaired adolescent by mouthing the words. The hearing-impaired adolescent reads the lips of the helper and then answers the friend directly.

It is also possible for a family member to simply play the role of secretary. In this case the "secretary" acts as intermediary for the hearing-impaired and normal hearing friends, making plans or providing messages on the basis of what they say. The problems around using the telephone are probably the most significant interferences for the hearing-impaired and hearing adolescents who want to develop a meaningful friendship. The problems are not insurmountable if the motivation to solve them is present.

The hearing-impaired adolescent need not be lonely in the mainstream, if he has enough self-esteem and self-confidence to reach out to potential friends and enough wisdom to choose them wisely. Some hearing people are endowed with the interest to be friends with someone who has a hearing problem. Finding such people and learning to give to them in return can result in a balanced and gratifying relationship between hearing and hearing-impaired adolescents.

Mindy, the self-sufficient hearing-impaired woman of whom I spoke before, and Stephanie come to mind. Both are in the mainstream. Mindy has many more relationships within the community of the deaf. However, she moves between the two groups, has romantic relationships with both hearing and hearing-impaired men. She also has many close platonic male and female hearing friends with whom she socializes regularly.

Stephanie seems to have developed the bulk of her social relationships within the hearing community. However, she has kept her friendships with the hearing-impaired friends she had as a child and adolescent. Although she is a member of the mainstream, she has not lost her links to members of the hearing-impaired community.

Conclusion

We have passed through the developmental hurdles from infancy through adolescence with a focus on fostering the fullest possible growth along the way. It is to be hoped that we will have done a good enough job in helping our child work out the challenges. If so, there is a very strong possibility that the developmental tasks will be accomplished by the end of adolescence. Then we can take great pleasure with our child and with ourselves. We have contributed to the development of a human being who is on his way to becoming a self-sufficient, self- confident, self-respecting young adult.

John K. Duffy, Ph.D., giving, wise, energetic and
affectionate, shown here with two of his protegés,
Kim Passero (left) and Stephanie (right).

Chapter X

Life as a
Hearing-Impaired Person:
Stephanie Speaks

I am one of many thousands of hearing-impaired people who has experienced many obstacles, challenges and successes. From my experiences you too may discover ways to help someone you love who is also hearing impaired.

When I was a baby I think I must have been fascinated by moving lips. Somehow, I knew there was something important coming from the lips of my parents and other people. Before anyone even knew of my hearing problem, I learned to use my eyes to speechread. Eventually, I got my first hearing aids, and these enabled me to hear the world through sounds, not just through silent moving lips. My lipreading ability expanded as I also learned to read the facial expressions that went along with speech. These abilities would become very powerful assets in my learning to function entirely on my own.

Another way I was helped to hear, was learning to read and write when I was very young. I did not really understand all the fuss about letters until one day in nursery school. I had painted a picture and my teacher wanted me to write my name on it. Since I was accustomed to writing by the time I entered nursery school, I wrote "Stefan $\varepsilon\varepsilon$ " in the letters of the Initial Teaching Alphabet. The Initial Teaching Alphabet was unfamiliar to my teacher who showed me another way to spell my name. This was the way I had been registered in the school: "Stephanie." She explained that the 'ph' she wrote sounded like the 'f' I wrote. My ' $\varepsilon\varepsilon$ ' sounded like her 'ie'. I have been spelling my name her way for a very long time. I began to see with my eyes through the written letters on a page what I could and could not hear.

My hearing aids have always been very important to me. I wore body aids for a long time with wires running up from the two small boxes that made two bumps on my chest through the harness which secured them to my body under my clothing. During the early years I was proud of my aids, and I learned to take pretty good care of them. I don't think I was self-conscious about them, because until I was nine years old I lived on a street with a bunch of kids I grew up with who accepted me and didn't seem concerned about my aids or my hearing impairment.

My devotion to my body aids did not last forever. When I was about nine, I told mom I wanted to wear behind-the-ear aids. It was becoming a hassle to wear body aids. This was at a time I was beginning to sense that I was different from the rest of the people in my school. Being different did not seem to cause me problems during my early years in nursery school and kindergarten, where I remember feeling accepted. But feeling different as I grew older has been the most difficult part of being hearing impaired. Kids my age were taking notice and had started to point their fingers at me. I could hear in my mind that they were saying, "See those wires coming from her ears." At those times I wanted to go home to my old neighborhood and my friends who didn't seem to care what I had on my ears.

Anyway, I was taken to Dr. Duffy, my audiologist, who said he would set me up for a trial period during the summer with a pair of behind-the-ear aids. I was very eager to do this. I got the new aids just around the time we were leaving for a camping trip. I put them on before we left and the minute I turned the volume control I knew something was wrong. I wasn't hearing as much as I was used to hearing with my body aids. Although I ignored this disappointment, I did take my body aids along, just in case.

I wore the behind-the-ear hearing aids for two or three days. Finally when we were driving in the car, I broke through my disappointment. I told mom that these aids weren't working right for me, because I just couldn't hear as well as I did with the body aids. Right then and there I changed back to my old aids. I think I wasn't totally devastated, because it was my own decision. But I was sad. I just decided I would have to wait until science improved the technology.

I did wait a few more years until I couldn't live with the body aids any longer. At the age of thirteen I made the switch; it really had to be done. I was a maturing teenager and during these years many people take notice of little things about which one is sensitive and can really make you feel less of a person. With the body aids I may have heard more, but the social and emotional strain was just too high a price for me to pay.

To this day I don't fool myself. There is something different about my speech, and I have always known this. But it is not **that** different, so people usually have an easy time talking with me. Often when people first meet me, they ask what country I come from. I really enjoy this, because some people just think I have a foreign accent!

I am glad I could stay as long as I did with body aids, because when I switched I missed a lot of sounds that I had been able to hear with the body aids. For a long time I tried to hide the new aids also, because still I didn't want anyone to see that I was different. Today I wear very powerful behind-the-ear aids. Anyone can see them; it doesn't matter to me any more. I'm older, and I've accepted my hearing aids as being an undeniable and necessary part of my life. But I have noticed that while I would encourage anyone who is hearing impaired to try to wear the more powerful body aids for as long as possible, I would not be able to bear the thought of wearing them again today. I am really grateful for developments in technology that have made behind-the-ear aids more powerful. I do think though that at the beginning, when a baby or a little kid is first learning about sound, speech, and language, the best aids should be chosen, no matter how visible or what type they may be.

I spent a lot of time playing in my neighborhood with my friends. I fitted in and could do whatever they could and more. Maybe that is why in some ways my friend Laura and I who were the oldest were the leaders. We were an active group climbing trees and the jungle gym which was in my backyard, riding our bikes all over the neighborhood, sharing snacks. The fun I had during those early years was non-stop, and I remember not wanting to come in for dinner.

I think I played as hard as I could, because mom and I always sat down to practice my speech almost everyday. It wasn't easy for either of us to get me to make all my problem sounds like 's,' 'ch,' 'sh,' 'st,' 'j,' 'sts.' I know we both got frustrated during these practice sessions. Mom had to have potato chips there for me as reinforcement. That was how I got paid when I was little for my hard work. I guess all that practice paid off in ways other than potato chips, because today I speak exceptionally well and really don't feel self-conscious about my speech or my language.

I was often pretty frustrated, whether I was working with mom or the speech therapist. Since I was a pretty good kid, I didn't give anyone a very hard time. It was almost as if I closed out all my feelings in order to make myself sit through all these tough times as patiently as I could. I just held back most of my angry feelings. I think now I should have talked about my anger and frustration right then and not have waited until I was much older to really discuss it. I don't know if I would have been able to. But I didn't take the opportunity, and it was not given to me until later in my adolescence.

In the summer of 1974 when I was almost ten, my family moved from Queens, New York to Great Neck. I thought I was into the move and the new house and happy about it. I really didn't allow myself to feel its impact until I began school that fall. I had left behind the friends I had from the beginning of my life, because my parents wanted a new house and a better education system.

By the start of school it seemed like I had made a very big sacrifice. I met a new group of kids who seemed different and very smart. Even though they accepted me, I just didn't feel comfortable. I will never forget the wonderful opportunity I had that very first week to meet and become friends with many people. After school all these kids stood around me, asking me for my address and phone number.

I honestly couldn't understand why, and I behaved in a distant sort of way, pretty obnoxious, I would say now.

In those days I seemed to lose much of my self-confidence and withdrew. I didn't speak as much as I had before. I turned inward to my own world. I spoke much more with the teachers, as if I believed they could understand my words more easily. I lacked a close friend and became very lonely.

I believe I separated myself, because I felt different. I was angry about being different. These kids seemed so smart and had such an easy time of it. I was angry, because I had to work very hard to make it in the regular school. But most important, and this is something which has taken me a long time to admit, was my inability to be comfortable with one friend at a time. And "one friend at a time" was the way it was in Great Neck for ten-year-old girls.

I, however, had always been friends in a group, and the group did mostly physical activities. In this new community where the kids lived far apart, kids made play dates, often by telephone. This in itself was an immediate problem, because I couldn't use a telephone. Then when they got together, they spent time inside their houses **talking**, not out in the neighborhood running, climbing, and riding bikes. I was just not ready for this social scene. It would take a long time for me to learn how to adjust to it. I would spend a lot of time feeling lonely and angry.

During this time mom stopped working with my speech, and I no longer went to a clinic for speech therapy. Instead I went for speech lessons in school. I had to leave the classroom with a few classmates who lisped and stuttered. Here I was not alone.

I'll never forget the day when my speech teacher said, "You will read the *Pledge of Allegiance to the Flag* over the loud speaker." I insisted that I would not. She was the type of women who didn't take take "no" for an answer, and I liked her a lot. I had no choice. I was sent home to practice the whole thing, which was typed on an index card with all the difficult words circled and underlined and specific sounds stressed. It was not long before I became enthusiastic, and I began to practice hard for it.

Then the day came. I stood in the speaker room, all the buttons were turned on for each classroom. I stood upright and spoke. It went so fast it was like a blur. All I could remember was walking back into my classroom and seeing my teacher clapping. And then I saw my classmates were clapping too in a standing ovation. Even today I feel very embarrassed by the whole thing, but also very happy for myself. From that day on I no longer sulked in my speech classes. I enjoyed working with my speech teacher for the rest of the year.

My speech teacher linked me up with another hearing-impaired girl that year. Linda was new in the community too. Linda and I were to become buddies all through junior high and high school. I think both of us were nervous about meeting, but it was a terrific event, because we supported one another throughout our school years. I finally felt I had a friend. We were placed in a few classes together. Linda had a mild-to-moderate hearing impairment in one ear and a very severe impairment in the other ear.

Linda was the type of person who asserted herself more than I did. She was the kind of person eager to see the world and very little could stop her. I began to pick up on some of her traits. Both of us stuck together and taught one another new things through our eagerness to learn. There was a good deal of competition between us. Our friendship which continues today was very important to me and helped me to grow.

Through Linda I met more hearing-impaired students who attended other Long Island high schools. This was a whole new world for me. They became my main friends, since I really never had allowed the "friendly" acquaintances I had made with the kids in my own school to develop into close friendship outside of school hours. There were many good times with the group of hearing-impaired students I had met.

Still, it was difficult for me to fit in easily, because I had been surrounded by the hearing world up to this time. Their ways were as new to me as the ways of the ten-year-olds I met when I first moved to Great Neck. Some of these new hearing-impaired friends were oral, but many went to the schools for the deaf and used sign language predominantly. I had never felt a personal need to sign and up to then didn't know anyone who needed me to sign to them. But now I was meeting people with whom I couldn't communicate, unless I learned sign language. I have tried many times to learn it. I took a course with my mom when I was in high school and a course in college. I had very limited skills because I did not practice.

I think it is difficult for me to use signs, because I haven't allowed myself to let it become a part of me. In recent times I have been letting myself go with the flow of it. I realize there is a part of me that has not wanted to be identified with signing, because I am an oral hearing-impaired person. But I feel certain that if I ever make hearing-impaired friends who needed me to sign, I would probably have an easy time learning the signing skills. In my second year of graduate school I will have another chance to learn sign language because it is part of my training.

In junior high and senior high school something had to be done with me. My parents, my itinerant teacher, and my physical education teachers would no longer allow me to stay on the side lines. And Linda, my friend, was not interested in being a wallflower. My Dad and my gym teachers in junior high school threw a softball mitt into my hands and said, "You are going to play ball!" No one was willing to accept my refusal, because I have very strong athletic abilities and some natural talent.

This was good because I participated in athletics all through junior and senior high school. I pitched for the softball team, played basketball and volleyball, and hung out around the gym every day. My only problem was that I was a very slender kid and not as strong and aggressive as I am today. I have become a good tennis player and can give anyone a good game, if I get into it.

I stayed with the extra-curricular athletics program and was involved somewhat after school with the other students. But in reality I was not available. I didn't feel too many people spoke with me or allowed me the opportunity to be friends with them outside of school. But I must admit that I did not speak to too many people either, nor did I offer my friendship to anyone after school.

When I think back, I wish I could do my public school days over again. It would definitely be very different, since I have gained back much of the self confidence I think I left behind in the neighborhood in Queens at the age of nine. Today it would be easier to make friends and be a friend. And, with more confidence I would not have tolerated being lonely.

It would be misleading if I did not tell you about some of the social pleasures I **did** have during my high school days. I had been going to day camps all my life, and I wasn't lonely during the summers. I did pretty well, in fact, because I was in a group and the activities were very physical and arts-and-crafts oriented.

The summer of my fourteenth year my mom and dad encouraged me to attend sleep-away camp, and I remember giving them a very hard time. I was really concerned about privacy and group living, but

I didn't tell them. But I didn't tell them much about anything. Getting me to say anything about my feelings was like pulling teeth. So I was just being negative about going to camp.

However, my mom, who rarely gives up, managed to get me to open my mind. She persuaded me to "gather information" about the camp my sister was interested in attending. She got the names of some campers who had been to the camp and were intending to return. She got me to agree to talk with each of them. Then she set up meetings in restaurants in their towns. I remember sitting there chatting with three different girls at three different times, feeling so young and unsure of what camp had to offer me. I asked questions about privacy, waking up in the morning, the other campers, the activities, etc. The more I spoke with these girls, the more appealing camp became.

Finally I met Judi, the last of the campers with whom I was supposed to meet. We were invited to her apartment in New York City. I met her parents who were very involved with the camp. They were very caring. So I finally decided to go for at least part of the summer.

In the months before camp Judi corresponded with me, and I was thrilled to know that someone cared about me. It was easy to communicate by mail. There was no telephone obstacles to overcome. Occasionally we got together, and I would open up and talk about my thoughts and feelings. Judi enabled me to begin to feel self-confidence and discover what being comfortable in a relationship is about.

When I arrived at camp that first day, I saw Judi from the window of the bus, waiting eagerly for me to get off so she could welcome me with open arms. I remember feeling so safe knowing that Judi was there for me that entire summer. I had been placed in the bunk with the girls I had already met, and it was good to see their familiar faces. I was nervous, but not as nervous as I could have been if had had not known anyone. There were many new faces, and I was ready to make new friends.

I haven't seen Judi since 1984 when she left Cornell after her freshman year to go to Israel where she lives. But, we communicate by mail. Although we are far apart I still feel very close to her.

When it came time to apply to colleges, I was once again in a predicament about going away or staying home. But by the time I was sixteen I was beginning to notice that my dilemma, as well as many of my other problems, was a direct result of my lack of confidence. Something was happening to me. Camp had been good, and I remembered

I had been resistant at first. I began to see that I was getting in the way of my own happiness because of my insecurity.

I decided to go away to school. After visiting several schools, I chose Ithaca College. I applied for an early decision admission, and I was accepted! I was very proud of myself. I was scared, but also eager to go. I spent a lot of money on things to take to school. It was a way of trying to insure I would be happy living in the dormitory.

From the moment I arrived on campus and throughout the four years at Ithaca I grew in many different ways. I did well academically and was graduated with a Bachelor's degree with a major in health education and a minor in psychology. This required that I did student teaching, which was a very big challenge. First, I taught high school students and then junior high students. I learned what it takes to be an effective teacher. It was not easy. The students accepted me, and we all adjusted to my speech without difficulty. I worked hard to speak better in front of large groups. By asking thoughtful questions and trying to make my lessons fun, I discovered how to get the class involved in the lessons. And we really had fun.

The academic work in college and graduate school has not been too hard to manage. I have finally learned to make sure everyone in class knows who I am and that I am hearing impaired. I have explained to the professors the first day of class that I need to see their faces when they speak. That is all I tell them at first. I have felt too many guidelines would be a burden for them. I have asked for the minimum at first because I know, if necessary, I can ask for more.

I have checked out each class and asked people I thought would be competent and reliable notetakers to put my carbon paper under their notes. These people have been supportive and helpful. They have enabled me to follow what the teachers are saying. Notetakers have provided the most important special help I have received beginning in junior high and continuing through graduate school. Because of them I don't worry about taking notes. I just listen and speechread the teachers.

During my years at Ithaca College I decided to take myself to the Speech and Hearing Clinic on campus for speech therapy. This time it was my choice and the frustration was gone.

College was the place where I grew up. But I couldn't do it all by myself by just being there. The relationships I developed were very important. I have seen that I have been influenced by some of my good friends and that I have adopted some of their characteristics also. One of those important people in college was Brad, whom I met early in my freshman year. He was my boyfriend through our first year. He taught me how to enjoy life, to relax, to reach out to another person, to talk freely, to be myself, and to be different and not afraid to show it. I became a fairly friendly, nice, warm, and outgoing girl. I also became stronger and began to study who I really was and what I had to offer to others. Finally, I was beginning to discover the importance of one-to-one relationships.

Brad helped me become more of the person I am underneath. But I limited myself to him only, and in some ways limited my social life. Everyone knew "us," but did not know me separately. After a year of living in the same dorm and being with each other every day, we broke up and eventually became friends for the remaining three years.

In the next three years I went from developing important one-to-one relationships with individual girlfriends and relationships with small and large groups of girls. We roomed together, vacationed together, traveled together, studied together, laughed and cried together, grew together, and graduated together. I spent my college days getting to know people and learning to be a friend.

Since high school and during college, there have been many wonderful and not-so-wonderful guys in my life. I have had many long-and-short-term relationships. Some of the guys were hearing impaired. However, most of my relationships have been with hearing guys. I am not interested at this time in a serious relationship, because I realize that I need to know who I am before I can share myself with anyone else.

College opened up a new world for me. I am still processing the excitement of these past four years. One thing is certain, I really changed. I pat myself on the back for making it the best four years of my life. I learned to make friends, be a good friend, assert myself, be in the flow, teach kids health education, be friends with professors, get some academic knowledge, be more contented with myself, and be by myself too.

Being in the academic mainstream throughout my education has been difficult. I have had to work extra hard to meet the requirements and get decent grades. Sometimes, I did not succeed even though I had worked hard and I became very discouraged. There were times when I wanted to quit. But I made myself think positively at these times and fought the frustration. I believe this is the way it is for any disabled person, no matter what their particular disability may be.

I admit it bothers me that others can put in two hours of study to my three hours, go out and play, and frequently do better. However, the extra work is a necessity, and it is the reason I have succeeded in meeting the academic demands undertaken by my own choice. The success that results from my hard work is a wonderfully rewarding experience and keeps me willing to work hard. It has taken me a long time to accept the fact that I must be ready to give more than the average person. I wouldn't have made it to Tufts otherwise. I know that I can get my master's degree as long as I am willing to put out a lot of effort. This is part of being hearing impaired and being in the mainstream. It is not easy, but I want it this way.

Through the years I held various jobs. I worked in a supermarket, in a library, on an assembly line in a factory, and in a camp as a counselor for retarded people. After my summer at the Human Resources School working with severely physically disabled students as an aide in the Occupational Therapy Department, I knew that I wanted to study Occupational Therapy in graduate school. I was accepted by Tufts University School of Occupational Therapy in Massachusetts where I have an apartment that I share with my cat, Teddy. My friends visit frequently. I feel secure living on my own and being responsible for myself.

I was scared the first day I started at Tufts. I sat among a group of seventeen people who were my classmates and my new "family." As a group we were varied. Some were much older than I, others were making a significant career change, still others had a great deal of experience, and some had none. At first I felt like a mouse, small and scared, until I began to realize that these people in the program also felt insecure.

Very quickly we became friends. My apartment became my new home and Boston, my new city. I have made many new and wonderful friends. I have learned to study much harder than ever before. I have begun to play tennis actively with people that I met while in graduate school. I have taken myself all over Boston: to the museums, movies, through Harvard Square, etc. It takes guts to go as far as I did. I know that if it weren't for my new and old friends, I don't think I would have been as comfortable as I am living in Massachusetts.

One of the reasons it is so significant that I am living alone now, is that I do not have anyone to help me in case I have a problem. But

I have devices that make life more secure. I have a bed alarm that shakes the bed and wakes me up in the morning. However, most of the time the clock in my head gets me up just before the bed shakes. I have a fire alarm, but I need to wear my hearing aids in order to hear it. My neighbors are aware of my hearing impairment so I can depend on them in an emergency. I have a caption device on my television so that I can get the news and weather report in the morning.

I have a telephone light that lights up each time the phone rings. I am dependent upon this light when I do not wear my hearing aids. I also have an amplifier on my telephone that enables me to speak to anyone who calls. Before I moved into my own apartment, the telephone was a big frustration. I could only use the phone effectively if it was a TDD call, which meant I could type my part of the conversation and the other person could type his or hers. When I would speak to a hearing person, I needed someone to report their message by setting up a third phone or turning up the amplifier so my helper could hear. This person would mouth the speaker's message and I would respond.

It is not a comfortable feeling to have someone interpret for me. I always appreciated my friends' and family's willingness to interpret, but I really didn't like their being part of a two-way conversation. There was no privacy. Ever since I moved into my own apartment and have had no interpretors. I have had to learn to manage the phone. I have learned to listen and concentrate much better, so I can actually have simple conversations with success. I can make plans and give and receive some information. I have learned to use my hearing and my creativity to make the phone work for me. Although I can use it only in simple ways, it is still great!

It took me a long time to convince my parents to buy another TDD so I could give it to a friend. I finally got my "loaner" TDD before leaving for Massachusetts. The very first day I gave it to a classmate, in case I needed her help or she needed mine. She still has it, and we use it every day. Sometimes I give a friend her number to call, because she is willing to get a message to me.

All in all I have learned there are ways to get around most of life's difficulties. Whenever I experience the successful solution to a tough problem, I think about all the challenges of the past that got me down and what a waste of time that was.

Even though I have not spoken much about my mom, dad, and sister, without them I definitely would not be where I am today. My mom has been the major influence in developing who I am today. But without my dad being there for my mom, supporting her and having faith in us, my mom and I could not have been that successful. There is a strong bond between my sister Danika and me. We have a lot of values in common, and we have become the best of friends. I expect we will always be friends throughout our lives. My sister has a TDD, and she communicates with me from Duke University in North Carolina where she goes to school.

If I had the opportunity to begin again and live through my earlier years, I would certainly change one thing. I would have tried to express more of my feelings. I think this would have made my life easier, because I would have been able to find out earlier why I was so withdrawn. Then I would have tried to overcome it.

It has taken me a long time to deal with being different and with my sensitivity to the reactions of others to my differences. Somehow being different has made me special which is just as much a part of my identity as my hearing aids, my hearing impairment, and my brown curly hair. Also what I have been able to learn about my identity is that I have talents, ideas, and knowledge to offer that are not only of value to me, but of value to others. And that makes me feel like I really belong!

Chapter XI

Growing Up with
My Hearing-Impaired
Sister:
Danika Tells Her Story

A little girl about eight-years-old walked slowly home from school thinking about how hungry she was and what she would make for her snack. It was one of those days, when she was sure the clouds were going to explode and water was going to come crashing down on the earth. But all that existed was a miserable drizzle and a dark sky.

The little girl increased her pace as she rounded a bend, the final stretch. There before her was the finish line -- home base, tall, strong, and secure. She hopped up the front steps, opened the screen door, stuck her hand in her pocket for her keys and realized she had forgotten them that morning. With relief she saw the light on in her sister's room. She rang the doorbell, her mind concentrating on the cookies she would soon be eating.

There was no response to the doorbell, so she rang again, and still her plea was met with silence. With the desperate realization that her sister had probably removed her hearing aids and would not answer the door, she began to ring the bell repeatedly in futile attempts to arouse her sister. She began to kick the door over and over again until she broke down, her body wracked with sobs. She fell to the ground and cried. In her heart she felt a pain worse than sorrow.

She sat quietly in her room trying to complete her spelling workbook for school. She knew the first person in her class to complete it correctly would receive a prize and special recognition from her first grade teacher. She concentrated and tried to decide if there were two "p's" or one in the word "stopping". She tried to suppress the urge to ask her mother. She could hear her mother's voice in the next room teaching her sister to talk: "'St' say 'st' just as in Stephanie." She could picture her mother gazing intently at her sister, while moving her hand near her lips in a way that coordinated with the sound her mother was trying to help Stephanie make. Every so often she was distracted by the laughter that accompanied a successful sound and the crunch of a potato chip or by the frustrated cry of her sister who would rather have been watching "Laverne and Shirley" on TV.

Spelling the word "neighbor" was presenting a problem. She slipped off her desk chair and worked her way into her sister's room. She wanted to ask her mom to sing her the "i before e" rule. She entered the room just in time for an "s" struggle. Stephanie's "s" sounded more like a "d". She watched her sister's face wrinkle in frustration. Suddenly Stephanie's eyes caught sight of her standing with her spelling workbook in hand. Stephanie began to scream at her, "Get out of my room!" Dejected, she turned and walked away.

"Happy birthday to you, happy birthday to you. Happy birthday dear Danika, happy birthday to you." Now make a wish and blow out the candles. "Please God, let me be able to fly and let Stephanie be able to hear."

She sat on her new bicycle. Today her friend had come over to play. In the distance they saw Stephanie and her friend. They all converged on the driveway, and she yelled, "Hey Steph, what are you doing?" Stephanie replied that she was going to make a snack with her friend, and they proceeded into the house.

She couldn't help thinking how fine Stephanie's speech sounded. Then suddenly she felt like she had been stung by a thousand bees, because her friend asked what was wrong with Stephanie's voice. She answered, "Nothing. She always sounds like that," and quickly rode ahead on her bicycle yelling, "Hey look what I found over here." And her friend quickly lost interest in her previous question.

She sat in the library's recreation room going through her training to become a peer counselor to the incoming freshmen. The man with the mustache and warm blue eyes asked, "If you could change anything about yourself what would it be?" Immediately she thought of her physical imperfections. Then she began to think about her sister. If she could change anything, she would want to give her sister the ability to hear. Suddenly two tears filled her eyes and in the frustration of realizing the impossibility of her wish, they rolled down her cheeks, the first in a flood of a thousand more.

They strolled down a cobblestone street on a beautiful summer day. All around them were people walking, talking, buying, selling, and eating. It was a day when people seemed to be smiling, or perhaps she perceived it that way, because **she** was smiling inside.

They entered a small boutique. Anyone describing them would say that they were two happy young girls. She looked through the clothing, Stephanie periodically approaching her and asking for her nod of approval on particular items. They made their purchases and walked to a nearby cafe. They decided what they wanted to order, and when the waitress approached, she told her what they wanted. They were together not yet as equals, but at the beginning of a relationship. She was sixteen, and Stephanie was twenty.

Growing with Stephanie

Last week I had a conversation with Stephanie and as I hung up the phone and unplugged the TDD, I realized we had become friends. In this one instance she had finally assumed the role of the big sister.

She had given advice, and I had listened. She is twenty-two, and I am eighteen.

I have felt many emotions in regard to Stephanie. Until very recently, I had not analyzed or even recognized my feelings. Our family practiced the "do not dwell on Stephanie's hearing impairment" theory. We preferred to think of how we could help Stephanie become a non-handicapped person, and then went about doing what we believed would be helpful. Very rarely had I ever consciously thought about her hearing impairment, except when my friends or others made an issue of it. These were the times that I was forced to face society's perceptions of Stephanie as being "different" or "special". And then, I felt an agonizing hurt, which made me feel more determined to help her overcome whatever the difficulty was.

I do not believe this was the wrong approach. It may even have been largely responsible for Stephanie's success. Stephanie has proved that she can live the life of a non-handicapped, hearing-impaired person.

Sometimes I think Stephanie succeeded in order to prevent my parents and me from being disappointed for her and for ourselves. Her success feels like a gift she has shared with us. I know that I aim to please the people I admire and respect to keep the flame of their admiration for me constantly burning. I think Stephanie has this desire also. The many people who have helped her through the years (not just her family) have reason to feel great pleasure.

Stephanie has experienced life both in the oral, hearing-impaired world and life in the signing, hearing-impaired world. She studied sign language and has friends who use sign language primarily to communicate. She chose to use her voice rather than her hands. She has chosen to be an oral, hearing-impaired person. As a result, I believe she has had much greater opportunity to learn from her environment.

Stephanie has had to train herself to adapt to the environment so that she can function as a non-handicapped person. I observe how she is able to participate in group conversations in which both her eyes and ears must shift from speaker to speaker so that she does not lose contact with the group. This is very hard for a hearing-impaired person. In my experience with her hearing-impaired friends, most of them do not even try to stay involved in the group conversation.

Stephanie has cultivated an awareness of the many emotions possible in a given situation. Consequently, she can predict the type of responses people tend to make. She can effectively follow the language in real situations, on television and on movie screens using all her language skills and her pretty dependable intuition.

Stephanie is incredibly determined to accomplish her goals. She developed her determination as she mastered her speech and language. I believe Stephanie has been able to succeed so well because she was determined to meet the difficult challenges for adjustment to the hearing world.

As Stephanie's sister I have learned that boundless patience is a virtue that would be wonderful to have at all times when dealing with a hearing-impaired person. But I do not believe that endless patience is necessarily a healthy or realistic condition for either person. There are inevitable frustrations on both sides.

I have finally learned that it is okay to acknowledge my frustration and to express my annoyance. For example, if we fought over when I could help her with a phone call, it was okay. I wanted to help her, because she could not do it herself. But I could not jump every time she needed something because I felt bad for her or guilty that I was able to do it and she was not. It was okay for Stephanie to kick me out of her room when she was frustrated while practicing her speech sounds.

What makes our relationship healthy is that we acknowledge that there are special adjustments that have to be made because Stephanie is hearing impaired. In making these changes we can be honest about our very normal emotions. Stephanie has taken my abuse, and I have taken hers. We both know that our expectations of each other are often hard to fulfill. We understand each other's frustration and anger. We have a genuine respect for one another because we appreciate each each other's strengths and we understand each other's weaknesses.

A very young child with a hearing-impaired sibling will have to face a multitude of feelings including sadness, embarrassment, and guilt. A child in this position needs help to learn to deal with these feelings so that they are not expressed in an unkind or hurtful way. I was once this child. As I grew older and became more mature, I began to understand that my sister is really "special" because her accomplishments are extremely special. I am very proud of my sister. I am finished being sad, embarrassed, and guilty. Now I just smile in amazement.

Chapter XII

The Man in Her Life: Father Tells His Story

It is a special moment for every man when he looks at his new-born child and imagines what the future will bring. It is a brief interlude of pleasure and excitement. The dream in that moment is about his child and anticipation of the significant events of the early years. He imagines his child beginning to walk, learning to ride a bicycle, entering nursery school, beginning the first grade, entering high school and wonders what his child will be like at the age of high school graduation. It is a feeling for life that supercedes all the other realities that confront us when a newborn arrives. Instinctively we want our child to be especially beautiful or handsome, talented, bright, and a high achiever. All of these thoughts raced through my mind during that moment when I fantisized about Stephanie and her future.

When I saw her at the window of the hospital nursery for the first time, her face was all red and her head was somewhat squashed. My joy was mixed with concern. Then I looked at the other babies in the nursery and realized that Stephanie looked like all the other infants. That first time I observed Stephanie was one of the highlights of my life. There is nothing quite comparable to observing the child you have helped to create. It was awesome. I wanted to shout. I wanted to leap as high as I could, and at the same time, I wanted to cry. There is my seed, there is a part of me. I wanted never to lose touch with that memory and that moment.

Parenting is difficult. It is even more difficult to hold onto those precious moments and recollections as we raise our children to adulthood. I believe those moments must be recalled throughout our lives and be an integral part of the love we have for our children as we teach and guide them, and cope with their problems as they grow to maturity.

I have a recurrent memory of pushing the carriage along the avenue on a Saturday morning, when Stephanie was about eight months old. It is a vivid memory. It was my moment to look into the future. I recall imagining how Stephanie would develop, what she would look like at the age of twenty-one. I pictured myself playing ball with her and her friends. She would be a good athlete. She would be popular. I thought about all the different things I would share with her. I would teach her to be athletic. She would be a good student.

As I walked, I observed her standing in the harness in the carriage, smiling and jumping. I was experiencing that super high that brings together the impact of fatherhood and the excitement of anticipating your child's growth. It is a wonderful memory that comes to mind whenever I have been with Stephanie at the important crossroads in her life.

Stephanie was a typical infant. She cried, she screamed, she laughed, she was very playful. I loved to cuddle her and hold her high over my head. I was also available for diapering and feeding and the night-time rocking.

When she was about seven or eight months and beginning to stand and walk holding onto the bed, the dresser, or the wall, I played a game with her. She had plastic model animals. A dog, a cow, a lamb, a bear and others. We kept them on a shelf at her level, and she played with them frequently. On weekend mornings she would be playing in the bedroom, and I would ask her to bring to me the bear or the dog. She would go off and return shortly with the correct model. Of course I cheered, and she was overjoyed. I had no idea she could not hear me and was reading my lips!

Stephanie communicated quite well with me. She was expressive, curious, and interested in what she observed around her. The sounds she made were descriptive. I reinforced language as everyone does when a child begins to make sounds. I still had no idea Stephanie could not hear me and that she was effectively lipreading.

Throughout these early months, however, Stephanie's mother expressed great concern about Stephanie's failure to respond to the dog barking, the doorbell, the radio, and other sounds. I discounted her concerns. Stephanie behaved so normally, reacted so well in my conversations with her, I could not conceive that she could not hear. However, I knew that her mother needed encouragement from me to actively investigate her concern about Stephanie's hearing.

At the same time she did manage to get the pediatrician to perform some rudimentary tests. He placed a tuning fork adjacent to each ear. He did not observe a problem. However, he thought Stephanie's eyes were not exactly correct and sent us to an eye specialist. There was nothing wrong with her eyes.

I will never understand why pediatricians are so reluctant to refer infants for audiological examinations, when they are so quick to refer them to other specialists. Throughout the early years all the parents I met, who had concern about their child's hearing and consulted with their pediatrician, were never immediately referred to an audiologist for testing. Even today I continue to hear stories from parents and grandparents of young hearing-impaired children about how their pediatrician failed to recognize the problem and failed to refer them to an audiologist for a hearing evaluation at the beginning of their concern and their questioning.

One evening when I had just come home from my office, Stephanie's mother called me into the bedroom where Stephanie was asleep. She held in her hands two large pots. She asked me to observe and quickly smashed the two pots together making a terribly loud sound. Our dog began to bark. Stephanie did not flinch. Stephanie did not move. She did not react at all. Something was wrong. Stephanie was eleven months old.

I have thought about the events following that evening and have realized that I was not really an active part of the investigation process.

I should have been. Contact was made with the audiologist, Dr. Duffy. The testing was done. I was not there. I should have been. I was at the second testing done at another clinic by a former student of Dr. Duffy, who was indecisive about how Stephanie was responding to the sounds in the soundproof room. While we were in his office he called Dr. Duffy, and they conferred by telephone.

Dr. Duffy's recommendation was to invest in the earmolds. If Stephanie had hearing, the amplified sounds would be too disturbing, and she would more than likely pull the cords connecting the molds to the aids from the earmolds. If she did not instantly pull the cords from the earmolds, then her reaction to the sounds around her should be carefully observed. This recommendation made so much sense that I did not hesitate to agree.

I was not present when the aids were put on Stephanie for the first time. I should have been. I learned that Stephanie could not hear when her mother called me on the telephone and informed me about how Stephanie had reacted. I cannot recall even pausing for a moment to reflect on the meaning of this. I did begin to reassure my wife that we could handle this and that everything would be 'okay.' I should have been home with her and Stephanie and not talking over the telephone.

With all the memories I have of Stephanie I find it strange that I do not recall my first thoughts when it became apparent to me that Stephanie could not hear. I never thought about any aspects of having a child with a physical handicap, wearing hearing aids, and any of the life-long problems Stephanie would face. I never thought about whether the problem could be surgically corrected. In retrospect, it disturbs me that I accepted what I was told without question. I did not mobilize. I should have.

I knew that Stephanie's mother would dedicate herself to bringing language to Stephanie. She would do whatever had to be done. I do not know how I knew this, nor did I realize the enormity of the task. I do not recall ever really discussing a plan or a strategy to deal with Stephanie's problem -- our problem. I knew I would be helpful and supportive. I thought I would be equally committed to the job of teaching language, but in retrospect I did not know what committment really meant.

Now, after twenty-two years of experiencing the committment to Stephanie, I know what it is. Certainly, committment is being supportive, dedicated and helpful. In that sense I was committed to my wife. I was confident that she had the strength, the spirit, the creativity, and the depth of character to challenge Stephanie's hearing impairment, and succeed in bringing language to Stephanie. Her committment to Stephanie was steadfast. I know now that it must be an uncompromising dedication, because there is little room to bend to frustration, disappointment, discouragement, or any other self-defeating purpose. In that unyielding depth of committment there was tremendous power.

Stephanie's mother was committed to the natural development of language. The professionals who came in contact with her and with Stephanie knew that, whatever the challenge might be, her determination would accomplish the goal. Stephanie would speak.

What could I do for Stephanie? My primary goal was that she would be one of the regular kids growing up in our neighborhood. I did not want her to suffer the rejection that I pictured for all handicapped children. I believed, perhaps in a naive way, that if Stephanie was given a chance to develop her physical skills early in her life, it would give her a headstart on the other children. She would excel and thereby be more readily accepted by the group. Perhaps then her hearing impairment would not be a big issue.

As soon as Stephanie was walking, I was teaching her how to throw a ball and how to catch it. She could throw and catch quite naturally when she was very young and bat a ball well too. I taught her some gymnastics by balancing her, as she stood on my hands, and raising her over my head. Eventually she took gymnastics classes and did well in the various exercises. I was delighted to participate in these activities with her. These were the years when girls' athletics were just beginning to gain attention, and I was very proud of her athletic abilities.

I did not perceive of this as compensation for her hearing loss. I thought of it rather as a confidence builder. It was what I could give her to help her cope in the hearing world. In fact, in junior high school and high school Stephanie was able to actively participate in team sports and earn awards from the athletic department. The athletic training provided Stephanie with another dimension in her development that I know helped her a great deal to interact more comfortably with her hearing peers.

In retrospect, I do not think that this was enough. I always practiced my belief that she needed to function independently and had high expectations for her self-sufficiency. However, I do not think I was sensitive enough to all the issues that young people face today growing up in our society.

I can recall the times that I was insensitive to Stephanie's needs during her childhood and throughout her adolescence. I did not take into consideration the reality that she did have a profound impairment and required additional support. I failed to fully understand the day-to-day problems she encountered. She did not share these problems with me. I think she was reluctant to communicate her concerns and conflicts with me, because I had not shared my feelings about her with her and expected her to cope with her problems independently. I was seeing her as just another child, when in fact she was very special. It is important to recognize the need to teach our children to be independent. It is also important to acknowledge their disability and provide extra support for them.

I have often underestimated Stephanie. I think this attitude forced her to feel that she had to convince me continuously of her capabilities. I failed to tell her how special she really was and how much credit she deserved for her accomplishments. How foolish I was.

At the high school senior awards, I was surprised when Stephanie was granted the award for the hardest worker in the mathematics department. When her teachers in high school and college assured me that Stephanie was doing well, I really did not understand the extent of their admiration for her and what it meant about her as a person.

As a parent of two exceptional children -- a disabled child and a gifted child -- I have learned that the greatest disservice a father can do to his children is to withhold thoughtful and sensitive expressions of his feelings about them. When he is struggling with feelings of denial, guilt, embarrassment, and disappointment, he must be open to himself and try to understand the basis for these feelings. These feelings are very personal issues about his own adequacy and his connection to his children. It is important to focus on these uncomfortable feelings, put them into proper perspective, and deal with them constructively as they relate to the interaction with his children. Otherwise, like an infection that is not treated, these feelings can have a detrimental impact in his effective communication with them. It is not possible to hide feelings. They surface one way or another. Sometimes they arise in angry and hurtful outbursts; othertimes, in silent, despairing passivity.

During Stephanie's adolescence I was not as aware of her, her feelings, and my feelings about her, as I should have been. The love that I was eager to communicate and share with Stephanie was distorted by these unexplained feelings which caused us to withhold meaningful communication. It was unfair to expect Stephanie to love me, to cope with her impairment, and be comfortable with herself and others, if she sensed I was holding back, preoccupied, and denying in my relationship with her.

We parents of disabled children need to take a hard look in the mirror early in the lives of our children. It is not easy to be honest with ourselves. But, for their sake we really have no choice. There is no place for the denial or disappointment we may inevitably feel. If we cannot come to grips with these feelings and work them out in some reasonable manner, our children will have great difficulty working out their own disappointments and frustrations. Regardless of the obstacles, our children must be able to look to us for support, encouragement, confidence, and enthusiasm as they grow. If we are busy hiding our feelings from ourselves, we will be hiding ourselves from them during the time when our active presence is crucial for their well being.

I have been very fortunate. In spite of my not having done everything as correctly as I now realize I could have, Stephanie has become an outstanding person. Through the enormous efforts of her mother and the contribution of many helpful friends, family, and professionals, she is a statement of what a person can accomplish regardless of adversity and obstacles. I am very proud of her, and I know she is very proud of herself.

As "the man in Stephanie's life" it has taken me twenty years to understand some of the ways I have been part of her life. I could have been much more, but knowing that now has made me much more aware of what I will be in the future. The future is now!

Chapter XIII

Conclusion

The only way to avoid mistakes is to gain experience.
The only way to gain experience is to make mistakes.

I have given a plaque with these reassuring words to everyone in my family. I try hard to remember these thoughts when I am confronted by my mistakes. Therefore, it was with anticipation and apprehension that I waited for the chapters from Stephanie, Danika, and Alan which you have just read. I was very eager to learn what my family could teach you and me about raising hearing-impaired children who are well adjusted, oral, and successful. Intermingled with my eagerness was a large amount of anxiety and anguish about my mistakes, my errors of judgment, my omissions, etc.

You are probably just getting started. But I would guess that you have already engaged in your share of self-reproaches regarding how you have deprived, impaired, cheated, and otherwise hurt your child. When it comes to our children, especially our disabled children, we parents are very good at evoking our own guilt, whether well-deserved or not.

There is very little time to waste on remorse. The sadness from guilt is not a bad thing to feel, if it mobilizes you to put forth energetic and constructive efforts. However, guilt is not useful if it has a debilitating effect and interferes with our learning from bad decisions how to develop better ways of proceeding. Give up the guilt because it is a waste of your good energy. Recognize as a part of your being human that you should allow a margin for mistakes and errors of judgment.

I invite you therefore to learn from **my** mistakes. This will save you the trouble of making them yourselves and the anguish, if you do. You will help **your** hearing-impaired child, I will not have wasted **my** mistakes, and you can spend your mistake "allowance" in other ways.

Developing Special Skills

Since interpersonal relationships are apt to present the most stressful challenges to the hearing-impaired youngster, any support that you can provide to foster your child's social success is vital. Generate feelings of self-esteem by providing opportunities for your child to develop his inherent talents or skills. If your child can relate to other kids who have similar interests, he is going to be attractive as a source of information, a model to emulate, a partner to share with, a teammate to play with, etc. The talent or skill can be an 'open sesame' from which relationships can then be constructed.

It is not a small matter that Stephanie's father invested his energy to develop Stephanie's athletic talents into negotiable pitching skills. When it was hard for her to share with her peers in a verbal interaction because of her insecurity, she was able to relate athletically. She could go to the gym after school and practice, travel with the team to compete with other schools, play in intramural competition, and win recognition through athletic awards. If she could not have related through athletics, she would have come home after school, even more isolated, tense without some motoric release of the accumulated stresses from the day, and possibly developed serious emotional difficulties.

The photography skills she developed at a community program after school and at the fine arts summer day camp she attended from twelve to fourteen years gave her an opportunity for creative expression. This hobby became a meaningful occupation when she established her own darkroom and did her own developing. Later she was a counselor-in-training and worked in the photography program her second year at sleep-away camp. Her tennis lessons have made her a desirable doubles partner and enabled her to play singles games at the courts in our town and at school. She also used these tennis skills at Camp LeMar where she worked as tennis counselor for the campers.

We can find our child's potential talents if we look. Some children are artistically creative and would benefit from a fine arts program. Others have wonderful motor coordination that warrants participation in individual or team athletics. Others are gifted mathematically and could become "mathletes" instead of athletes. Still others would do well in the many new computer programs organized for children. Some have the grace and rhythm that warrants lessons in dance, music, gymnastics, or skating. Still others would do well in a club of stamp or coin collectors.

We need to help our children find something that makes them "special" in ways other than their hearing problems. Then we need to provide the opportunities to enable them to develop these potentials, enrich their lives, build their self-esteem, and help them make interpersonal contacts.

The Telephone

The telephone presents a special problem for the hearing impaired. I did not appreciate how much an adolescent's life depends on the telephone until too late. Nor did I recognize how dependent and angry Stephanie felt about needing our help every time she wanted to contact a hearing friend. I was aware of the intrusion into her privacy when I did help, but not aware enough. And I did not fully acknowledge how demanding and time-consuming it was to help her with the conversations.

Fortunately, we did not delay in purchasing the first TDD (telecommunications device for the deaf) for Stephanie, when they became commercially available. This enabled her to phone hearing-impaired friends who also owned TDD's. She could talk to them by phone through this telephone-typewriter machine. I feel relieved that we gave her this benefit.

However, I am very distressed that it took so long for us to purchase Stephanie's "loaner" TDD -- the one she is able to give to a friend with whom she wants to be in touch when they are apart. Once Stephanie had begun to reach out to her peers, she very much wanted to be in contact with them. So much important sharing, planning, and intimacy building is accomplished on the telephone, that the inability to use the phone easily can be a major frustration. It is an unnecessary frustration for any hearing-impaired person nowadays with the availability of the TDD.

I strongly urge every parent of a hearing-impaired baby to start saving immediately (pennies, nickles, etc.) for the purchase of a TDD, so that your child, when he is ready, will be able to talk with his friends who also have a hearing-impairment and a TDD. However, after the first one is purchased, start saving again for a second TDD. This one should serve as a loaner for those people your child will want to reach who are normal hearing and do not own a TDD. If and when your child goes away to school, you will need to purchase your third TDD. It is an absolute necessity in the day-to-day life of the hearing-impaired person.

Autonomy and Support: Striking the Balance

Throughout this book there has been an emphasis on enabling your child to become self-sufficient by providing support without undermining the spirit of autonomy, self-confidence, and self-esteem. However, there are times when it is necessary to provide support that may seem like an intrusion or overprotection. My husband has told you in Chapter XII of his emphasis on Stephanie's independence at the possible risk of withholding important supports. Neither infantilizing our children through overprotection nor abandoning them to their immaturity is desirable.

However, Stephanie did tell you in Chapter X about one place where I know I did not abandon her to make an immature, narrow-minded mistake in the name of fostering her autonomy. I see this as a case in point to illustrate the crucial balance. She mentioned our travels all over Long Island and into New York City to enable her to open her mind and learn about summer camp. I believed that going away to camp would be an important experience in her development, and I was determined to "make" her unlock her mind. When I read her comments, I realized it was probably one of the best things I ever did for her.

It was not easy to struggle with her stubbornness and her negativism. It was also not easy to explain to the camp administrator why I wanted the names of some returning campers her age. It was even harder to call the parents of these campers and explain my need for their assistance in providing information to Stephanie. Once through that hurdle I had to reach out and propose they allow me to take them to lunch so we could meet. After discussing this with the parents I had to present this to their daughters. I was asking a great deal of strangers, and it was very hard for me to do this. I felt presumptuous, anxious, very dependent on their good will, and humbled. I did not want to do it, but I did it anyway.

The actual meetings were very rewarding. Stephanie's sister Danika was more than willing to help with the conversations, since she understood the importance of this camp experience for Stephanie. This was not the first time she has helped Stephanie or me in a difficult situation. Each new girl we met was very helpful, and kind to Stephanie, Danika and me. I am very grateful to them because they enabled Stephanie to muster the courage to go to camp and derive tremendous benefits from her experience. Two of these girls from camp remain very close friends of Stephanie to this day. One is far away in Israel. The other now lives on the same street as Stephanie in Massachusetts.

Yes, I intruded. I forced myself and Stephanie to investigate a challenge. This type of incident was probably largely responsible for the way she tackles many of the problems she faces today: stubbornly, thoroughly, and courageously.

It is important to cultivate an "open door" policy for your hearing-impaired child. Welcome his friends (hearing and hearing-impaired) into your family. If possible arrange opportunities to have his friends join your child and/or your family in any experiences that have been planned. In addition, your relationships in your community with other families provides important interpersonal contacts for your child. If you are sociable yourself, it sets a friendly model for your child to imitate as well.

The Sibling

Many years ago I particpated in a film with Stephanie called *Early Decisions* which was produced by Dr. John Duffy at Brooklyn College of the City University of New York. My daughter Danika also participated in the film. Danika was included to demonstrate the importance of siblings as a source of stimulation and inspiration for the hearing-impaired child. It frequently happens that children can learn more effectively from children than from adults, which is one of the principles behind interage groupings in schools. Furthermore, the child who teaches has an opportunity to have his own knowledge reinforced.

Because Danika was exposed to my constant chatter and our "daily adventures," she started talking at about nine months. She was curious, bright, and playful and made a very good companion for Stephanie and assistant for me. Not only did Stephanie receive stimulation from me, she received it from Danika who was also a chatterbox.

Danika was also the little sister. I expected Stephanie to take responsibility for her. It meant that Stephanie had to guide, protect, instruct, play with, and "babysit" for her little sister. These responsibilities provided for extensive interaction between the two girls. They also contributed to Stephanie's developing the feeling that she was a very reliable person.

Danika's role in Stephanie's life was very important. Though distressed by Stephanie's hearing impairment, she moved toward Stephanie rather than away from her. She helped Stephanie become socially sophisticated in ways that only young people can help each other. Their conflicts, though nerve-racking, were not bloody and provided important opportunities to learn to conflict fairly and survive the conflicts. Danika has been responsible to Stephanie, and this has made her a very good friend, in general. She gave what Stephanie was unable to get from my husband and me in a manner that Stephanie was willing to take.

We need to recognize how important the other members of our family can be in helping a hearing-impaired sibling. Then we must remember to tell them how much we appreciate, love, and respect them for their help. The "normal" child in the family need not be the neglected child. This child can become an even more special human being for the experience of growing up with a disabled sibling.

Dealing with Immaturity: Add Another Year in Nursery School

Hearing-impaired children tend to be somewhat less mature than some of their hearing age-mates. A good deal of experience is missed because of the limited auditory input. For some children an additional year of nursery school can be very helpful. Growing up with children somewhat younger reduces the social and intellectual pressures of childhood. The somewhat more physically mature hearing-impaired child may be able to compete with greater success in the games of childhood that take place on the playground. This can give him an increased sense of confidence which is a very important advantage. The additional year will allow more time for intellectual and verbal maturity, as well, which may reduce feelings of inadequacy in the academic challenges of the classroom.

If your child is to be given the additional year, it is best to plan it during the early childhood years from nursery school through kindergarten. Then it becomes an opportunity to enhance your child's preparation. Instead of viewing the additional year as a statement of inadequacy, it is really a gift of another year of childhood along with some additional advantages.

To view your child as different and witness his struggle through his developmental years is an emotionally stressful experience for us parents. Some decisions we may have to make like adding another year to a school grade can be very difficult for us. We may execute these difficult decisions with apparent ease, but on the inside we may suffer great anguish. This brings us to the importance of having an assistant.

The Importance of Having a Special Helper

The children with whom I work often see me as their "friendly helper." Most of them are lonely and have adjustment problems. I regret not providing a helper for Stephanie when she was lonely and struggling to adjust. When she could have first benefitted from such help, it was still a time when many people felt that a person had to be emotionally ill to have a therapist. Today we are far more broadminded about providing therapeutic support as a means to cope with difficulties. Fortunately, we no longer wait until the emotional problem festers and a breakdown of functioning is imminent.

Furthermore, my family would have benefitted as a unit from having a family therapist or counselor throughout Stephanie's life. It is unfortunate we did not have one. Stephanie did not begin to have the benefits of meeting with a counselor until college. As a psychologist I should have known better. I have learned this too late. But fortunately she knows now that if she needs an impartial sounding board to share her ideas and feelings, she can have one.

I urge you to reach for the help of a therapist or counselor at the first signs of distress. If you are able, regular periodic visits for a mental health checkup is a good preventive idea, even when there are no critical problems. The role of the parent of a disabled child is a very challenging one. While it is enriching, exhilarating, expanding, and rewarding, it is also demanding, challenging, trying, frustrating, and exhausting. We humans can be very vulnerable, including those of us who feel strong and independent. Parenting our hearing-impaired child will enrich us, but it will wear on us, as well.

It is a wise idea to find a helper just in case you need to talk. There are psychologists, social workers, family therapists, and counselors from whom to choose. If you can find one acquainted with the impact of disability on families, so much the better. If you and your family make use of this person, you are apt to find yourself managing your life and helping your child more effectively.

I am inclined to wish you luck as we often say to people embarking on an important venture. However, I believe **people**, not luck, make things happen. Therefore, I wish you fortitude and boundless energy and the enduring memory of the words I have never stopped hearing. They have guided us through every obstacle and challenge we have encountered...they will guide you:

If one can do it, then another one can!

Resources
For Further Reading

The readings listed below are a small selection from the wealth of material available to help parents of hearing-impaired children arrive at vital decisions for their children and families. The list does not focus on books written for professionals, although professionals working with hearing-impaired children and their families will probably find them helpful.

For information about other publications your local library may list them in their card catalog. If your library has a limited catalog, you might wish to consult *Books in Print* under the subject index **deafness**. Titles that interest you could be borrowed by your librarian from another branch on inter-library loan.

The Alexander Graham Bell Association for the Deaf comes out with a Publications Catalog twice a year which lists its current publications. You can obtain this by writing to the Association at 3417 Volta

Place, N.W., Washington, D.C. 20007. This Association also publishes *The Volta Review*, an informative monthly journal on issues that concern hearing-impaired people and their families as well as professionals. You might want to consider membership in this Association and participation in its programs.

The National Association of the Deaf also publishes a list of books which you can obtain by writing to NAD at 814 Thayer Avenue, Silver Spring, Md. 20910. This Association publishes other material and offers other programs as well.

The *American Annals of the Deaf* is a national journal addressed to professionals who work with the hearing-impaired. You may want to review this journal to find out if you would like a subscription of your own.

Suggested Reading List[1]

Calvert, Donald. (1984) *A Parents Guide to Speech and Deafness*. Washington, D.C.: A.G. Bell Association for the Deaf. (Guidance to parents who wish to participate actively in helping their child to speak.)

Calvert, Donald. (1986) *Physicians Guide to the Education of Hearing-Impaired Children*. Washington, D.C.: A.G. Bell Association for the Deaf.

DuBow, Sy. (1984) *Legal Rights of Hearing-Impaired People*. Washington, D.C.: Gallaudet College Press. (Explanation of rights in the areas of education, employment, health care, and mental health.)

Erber, Norman. (1985) *Telephone Communications and Hearing Impairment*. San Diego, CA.: College-Hill Press, 1985. (Detailed

---

[1]When a title does not clearly indicate the book's contents, a brief description follows the listing.

213

discussion and specific instructions for the hearing-impaired on learning to use the telephone effectively.)

Ewing, A. and Ewing, E. (1971) *Hearing-Impaired Children Under Five: A Guide for Parents and Teachers*. Washington, D.C.: The Volta Bureau. (Specific recommendations to parents with inspiring examples of successful children in England.)

Ferris, Caren. (1980) *A Hug Just Isn't Enough*. Washington, D.C.: Gallaudet College Press. (Pictures and quotations from parents that deal with the choices and decisions parents must make for their hearing-impaired children.)

Froehlinger, Vera (Ed.) (1981) *Today's Hearing-Impaired Child: Into The Mainstream of Education, A Practical Guide for Teachers, Parents, and Administrators*. Washington, D.C.: A.G. Bell Association for the Deaf.

Griffin, Betty F (Ed.) (1980) *Family to Family*. Washington, D.C.: A.G. Bell Association for the Deaf. (Ten parents share feelings, ideas, and information about parenting their hearing-impaired children.)

Katz, L., Mathis, S., and Merrill, E. (1978) *The Deaf Child in the Public Schools*. Danville, Ill.: The Interstate Printers and Publishers, Inc.

LaPorta, R., McGee, D., Simmons-Martin, A., Vorce, E., Saaz von Hippel, C., and Donovan, J. (1978) *Mainstreaming Pre-schoolers: Children with Hearing-Impairment A Guide for Teachers, Parents, and Others Who Work with Hearing-Impaired Preschoolers*. Washington, D.C.: U.S. Department of Health, Education, and Welfare, Publication No. 78-31116.

Love, Harold (1970) *Parental Attitudes Toward Exceptional Children*. Springfield, Ill.: C.C. Thomas Publishers. (Identifies and addresses parental attitudes in order to encourage their self-understanding and to help them cope with important tasks in raising their children: especially Chapters 2 and 8.)

McArthur, Shirley. (1982) *Raising Your Hearing-Impaired Child: A Guide for Parents*. Washington, D.C.: A.G. Bell Association for the Deaf. (This is a practical guidebook written by the mother of two hearing-impaired children who is also a teacher of the deaf.)

Naiman, D.W., and Shein, J. (1978) *For Parents of Deaf Children*. Silver Springs, Md.: National Association of the Deaf. (Information about problems of daily living to help parents make important decisions.)

Neyhus, A. and Austin, G. (Eds.) (1978) *Deafness and Adolescence.* Washington, D.C.: A.G. Bell Association for the Deaf.

Nix, Gary (Ed.) (1976) *Mainstreaming Education for Hearing-Impaired Children and Youth.* New York: Grune and Stratton.

Northcott, Winifred. (1973) *The Hearing-Impaired Child in a Regular Classroom: Preschool, Elementary, and Secondary Years.* Washington, D.C.: A.G. Bell Association for the Deaf.

Rosenthal, R. and Jacobson, L. (1968) *Pygmalion in the Classroom: Teachers Expectation and Pupil's Intellectual Development.* New York: Holt, Rinehart, and Winston. (Discussion of the original research on the self-fulfilling prophesy, its power and importance.)

Scargall, Jeanne. (1973) *1001 Ways to Have Fun With Children.* New York: Charles Scribner's Sons. (One of the many available books with creative suggestions for activities that will offer opportunities for language stimulation for children and activities to stimulate your own creative ideas.)

Semple, Jean. (1970) *Hearing-Impaired Preschool Child.* Springfield, Ill.: C.C. Thomas Publishers. (Suggestions for parents to foster acquisition of speech and language and suggestions on how to manage behavior problems.)

Stern, Virginia. (1969) *Never Too Young.* New York: Lexington School for the Deaf. (Pictures and words illustrate how ordinary family life situations can be used to develop listening and language skills.)

Whetnall, E. and Fry, D.B. (1964) *The Deaf Child.* London: G. Heineman. (A technical, but informative and inspiring book from beginning to end. Although written fro physicians, it is, in the hands of the parents of the young hearing-impaired child, and incredible source of power in fostering the development of oral speech and language. Not to be missed: The publisher's note to the Preface (p. vi and vii) and Chapter 9.)

White, Burton. (1975) *The First Three Years of Life.* Englewood Cliffs, NJ: Prentice-Hall Inc. (A manual that provides many answers to questions about child development.)

Index

B

Babysitters, 143

C

Camp, 181-182, 206-207
Career-planning, 162-163
Child-centered, 53, 61
College education, 162, 182
Control, 106-110
Counseling, 14, 209-210
Creative arts, 80
Cued Speech, 94, 96

D

Decision-making, 108-110, 159-162
Disability, 20
Depression, 13, 17, 35-36, 111-114, 157
Decibel, 40, 41
Diagnosis, 6-10
    Audiologist, 7-10, 38
    Auditory-Brainstem-Response, 7
    Immittance audiometry, 6
    Informal-homemade hearing tests, 3-4, 7
    Otolaryngologist, 6-7
    Otologist, 6-7
    Physicians, 6-7
    Play audiometry, 8
    Sound-field audiometry, 8

E

Early Childhood, 146-149
    fears, 147-148
    decision-making, 146

Thanksgiving Day, 1987. Family games, mother center. A day of thanks and celebration for us. May there be many celebrations for you and your child too!